India's Politics

India's Politics

A View from the Backbench

BIMAL   JALAN

PENGUIN
VIKING

VIKING
Published by the Penguin Group
Penguin Books India Pvt. Ltd, 11 Community Centre, Panchsheel Park,
New Delhi 110 017, India
Penguin Group (USA) Inc., 375 Hudson Street, New York, New York 10014, USA
Penguin Group (Canada), 10 Alcorn Avenue, Toronto, Ontario, Canada M4V 3B2
(a division of Pearson Penguin Canada Inc.)
Penguin Books Ltd, 80 Strand, London WC2R 0RL, England
Penguin Ireland, 25 St Stephen's Green, Dublin 2, Ireland
(a division of Penguin Books Ltd)
Penguin Group (Australia), 250 Camberwell Road, Camberwell,
Victoria 3124, Australia (a division of Pearson Australia Group Pty Ltd)
Penguin Group (NZ), 67 Apollo Drive, Rosedale, North Shore 0632,
New Zealand (a division of Pearson New Zealand Ltd)
Penguin Group (South Africa) (Pty) Ltd, 24 Sturdee Avenue, Rosebank,
Johannesburg 2196, South Africa

Penguin Books Ltd, Registered Offices: 80 Strand, London WC2R 0RL, England

First published in Viking by Penguin Books India 2007

ISBN-13: 9-780-67099-929-3   ISBN-10: 0-67099-929-6

Typeset in Sabon Roman by SÜRYA, New Delhi
Printed at Thomson Press (India) Limited, New Delhi

To Minu

Let us make ready the beams of a tremulous heritage....

Contents

Preface   ix

Introduction   1

ONE   **The Rewards and Discontents**   39
         of Democracy
         Growth and Democracy   40
         Votes and Equity   46
         The Price of Liberty   52

TWO   **The Politics of Power**   65
         Political Opportunism   73
         Fiscal Disempowerment   78
         Public Dis-savings   83
         Excessive Centralization   90

THREE   **The Corruption of Politics**   98
         Causes of Corruption   102
         Costs to Society   113
         A Career of Choice   118

FOUR   **The Diminishing Role of Parliament**   **126**
        Taxation without Representation   130
        The Silences of Parliament   140
        Coalitions and Parliament   148

FIVE   **The Executive and the Judiciary**   **154**
        The Principle of Collective Responsibility 157
        The Politicization of Administration   165
        Separation of Powers   173

SIX   **The Reform of Politics in a   185
        Resurgent India**
        An Agenda for the Future   189

        Epilogue   **234**

        Index   **241**

Preface

This book is a sequel to a recent book *The Future of India: Politics, Economics and Governance*, published in 2005. As its title suggests, the present book is concerned with India's politics as it has evolved in recent years.

I have had the rare privilege of watching the working of India's politics as a nominated member of Parliament in the Rajya Sabha for more than three years. As I watched the proceedings, I also learnt that my understanding of India's politics was rather superficial, even though in my previous official capacity I had the benefit of frequent interactions with eminent political leaders in government and in the committees of Parliament. Participation in the work of Parliament from inside has been a different experience, sometimes highly satisfying and exhilarating but often worrisome. There is a lot going on below the surface in India's politics, which is not apparent to an outsider, but which could have substantial implications for the future of our country.

The primary purpose of this book is to convey, as best as I can, what I have learnt about India's politics from inside Parliament. The book also puts forward suggestions for political reforms in order to make India's democracy more stable, transparent and accountable. These proposals are practical and consistent with the parliamentary form of government. They are also in conformity with the intent of some recent amendments to the Constitution. I am conscious that the suggestions for political reforms made in this book are not likely to be easy to implement as they affect some established interests. My hope is that they will nonetheless inspire a broad public debate among concerned citizens, political leaders, experts, media and institutions of the civil society.

The views contained here are the personal views of a citizen-observer. I should emphasize that this book is not at all a 'memoir' or an account of what I said and what I did in the Rajya Sabha or elsewhere. As a nominated member, I am not affiliated with any political party. I am in Parliament just now, but not in electoral politics.

There is a fair amount of discussion in this book about the role of political leaders and political parties, some of which is not very flattering. My observations, such as they are, however, relate to our political system as a whole, and not to any particular party—large or small—or to any particular group of leaders in and out of office. I have consciously tried to deal with only 'systemic' issues, and not with any matter which is specific to a person, a selected group of leaders or a particular political formation.

India is fortunate in having leaders of high ability, competence and vision in government and Parliament. This is also true of political parties, each of which diligently try to serve the interests of its constituents. Collectively, however, the search for power and 'compulsions of coalition politics' in a diverse society, are increasingly the primary drivers of political behaviour.

The over-arching conclusion of this book, which I hope will be of particular interest to the reader, is simply that, over time, the power of leaders of political parties, particularly those of small parties, has increased substantially at the expense of ordinary members of legislatures and their constituents. With the emergence of multi-party coalitions as a regular form of government, and their relatively short life expectancy at birth, there is a palpable change in political dynamics which perhaps is not fully reflected in the original provisions of our acclaimed Constitution. Some of the recent amendments to the Constitution and other legislative enactments are in fact likely to increase political instability and encourage fragmentation of parties at the time of elections.

In a nutshell, without meaning to be provocative, I believe that if some of the emerging trends are not reversed, India's democracy *by the people* will become more and more 'oligarchic'—i.e. *of the few and for the few.*

I am grateful to K.D. Sharma and Satish Choudhary for their painstaking work in putting together the manuscript of this book for publication. I am also thankful to G.C. Khulbe for his assistance. The

publishers, Penguin Books, under the leadership of
Thomas Abraham, have been extremely supportive. I
am particularly grateful to Ravi Singh and Udayan
Mitra for carefully going through the draft and for
their editorial guidance. I alone am responsible for the
remaining errors.

New Delhi   **Bimal Jalan**
15 January 2007

Introduction

In the year 2007, when this book is being published, India will be celebrating the sixtieth year of its Independence. On 15 August 1947, when India became independent, in a celebrated and oft-quoted passage in his address to the nation, Jawaharlal Nehru said, 'Long years ago we made a tryst with destiny and now the time comes when we shall redeem our pledge, not wholly or in full measure, but very substantially. At the stroke of midnight hour, when the world sleeps, India will awake to life and freedom.' As we look back to that day, there is certainly much to rejoice in what India has been able to achieve. Sixty years ago, in view of India's poverty and diversity, not many political observers believed that Indian democracy would survive for long. It is gratifying to note that India's democratic system has not only survived but is universally regarded as a role model for peaceful transfer of power from one government to another after periodic elections.

Today, India is one of the few developing countries

in the world, where so many people—most of them very poor—cast their votes regularly in free and fair elections to elect their representatives. The birth of India's democracy after Independence was also unique. Unlike many other established democracies of the time, India's democracy came into being peacefully and without a revolution or rising by the people. It was put in place by its nationalist leaders; what was particularly remarkable was that all citizens were given the right to vote irrespective of gender, caste, creed, religion, income, occupation or level of literacy.

The Indian economy, which for quite some time—in the sixties and the seventies—was in the doldrums, has also recovered and shown rapid and steady growth since the beginning of the 1980s. The economy's potential for even faster growth is believed to be strong by experts all over the world. A view is gaining ground that India will become one of the dominant economies of the world by the middle of the twenty-first century. With a faster rise in per capita incomes, the curse of widespread poverty is also expected to disappear.

My purpose in writing this book, however, is not to praise India's democratic achievements or its economic prowess, which are now well appreciated all over the world. It is to remind ourselves that neither democracy nor economic resurgence can be taken for granted. Constant vigilance is indeed the price of liberty, and democratic processes and functioning—however satisfactory they appear on surface—cannot be, and should not be, frozen in time. The processes of governance, the distribution of power among different agencies of the State, the functioning of political parties, and the work of Parliament must be under periodic review. So far, in the fifty-five years since the adoption of its Constitution, India has adopted as many as 105 Amendments to the original Articles for one reason or another. The real issue now is not whether India's democratic electoral system has proved its sustainability, but whether it can be made to work better in the light of political developments over time.

The structure of this book is perhaps reasonably clear from its title and the list of contents at the beginning. The book is about the functioning of India's democratic politics, particularly after the beginning of the coalition era in 1989 as a *regular* form of government. The first five chapters deal with different aspects of the emerging political scenario— some of which are carry-overs from the past, and not necessarily related to coalitions, but some relatively new. There is considerable public and media discussion on each aspect taken separately—say political corruption or political opportunism—particularly when some high-profile event occurs, such as a change of government because of the defection of a coalition partner or charges of accumulation of illicit wealth by chief ministers and Union ministers. However, there is not sufficient appreciation of the fact that, taken as a whole, there have been some basic and fundamental changes in the functioning of India's democracy in recent years which can be ignored only at our peril. These changes are important enough to call for political reforms in the conduct of business in Parliament and other organs of the State. The last chapter proposes a ten-point programme of reforms, which are fairly modest and fully consistent with the parliamentary form of government and the 'basic structure' of our Constitution.

There are three basic reasons why, in my view, political reforms are now necessary despite all the positive developments in India's economy and its established traditions of electoral freedom. The first and foremost reason is the emergence of multi-party coalitions as a *regular* form of government. This is a relatively recent phenomenon (since 1989), and has significant implications for the working of India's democratic institutions. If multi-party coalitions are here to stay (as is likely), reforms are necessary to make them viable and more stable as per the original design of the Constitution. The second reason, which in some ways is connected to the emergence of coalitions as a regular form of government, is the question of internal security. There can be no doubt that an effective and stable administrative system under the supervision of political authorities is a *sine qua non* of providing adequate security to the people. Finally, in the economic sphere, a fundamental issue that needs to be considered is the role of the government in providing the minimum essential services to the poor in areas such as health, education, sanitation, and habitation. It is difficult to visualize a poverty-free and prosperous India without an effective system of governance. Let me briefly mention the main arguments why each of these reasons constitute a strong case in favour of political reforms.

All over the world, democracies are based on the principle of 'majority rule'. From time to time, in multi-party parliamentary democracies, the possibility of pre-election as well as post-election coalitions to acquire a majority and form a government is unavoidable. This is particularly true when a single party is well entrenched and has been in power for a long time, as was the case in India from 1947 to 1988 (with a brief interruption during the period 1977–79). As compared with single-party rule over a long period, it must be recognized that coalition governments also have some important advantages. Coalitions are generally more representative of different ideological interests, they are less dominated by a single individual or a coterie, and there are other in-built systems of checks and balances.

While, from time to time, coalitions are unavoidable and also have certain intrinsic advantages (as compared with permanent single-party rule), the global experience with the working of coalition governments has been mixed. A crucial pre-condition for successful coalitions is a shared commitment among all coalition partners to pursue a set of economic and social policies that are in the overall interest of the country. There may be ideological differences among the parties on the right, on the left and in the centre. However, once a coalition is formed, total commitment among all parties is necessary to support the decisions taken by their Cabinet under the leadership of the prime minister in a parliamentary form of government. All coalition partners are represented in the Cabinet, and differences among them should be ironed out internally rather than in public or on the floor of the House.

Thus, experience in countries with long-standing traditions of coalition governments shows that countries that have coalitions with internal harmony tend to be more stable and successful in achieving their national objectives than those that do not follow these rules. For example, Chile has had coalition governments for a long time which have been strong and long-lasting.[1] Coalitions have provided governments with a reliable majority, effective governance, and economic and political stability. Italy, on the other hand, which has also been ruled by coalitions of various types, has been much less successful in establishing a stable base of legislative support for its government in recent years. As a result, its economic and social performance has been adversely affected in comparison with those of other European countries. In between these two extremes, there are other coalitions (for example, in Brazil) that work well for some time but then disintegrate, leading to instability and policy incoherence.

Between 1989 and 2004, India had six coalition governments (including the short-lived thirteen-day coalition headed by Prime Minister Vajpayee in 1998, but excluding the government headed by Prime Minister Narasimha Rao during 1991–96). Among these, only the government formed by the NDA (National Democratic Alliance) in 1999 was in a position to complete its five-year term. The other five coalitions were short-lived, with varying majorities in Parliament. These unstable coalitions were supported by a large number of parties, on the left, the right and the centre of the political spectrum and there was no common platform or agenda except a shared opposition to the former ruling party. In addition to the above six coalitions, since May 2004, India has been governed by a new multi-party coalition under the UPA (United Progressive Alliance) banner led by the Congress party.

Compared with the earlier coalitions, the UPA coalition has some unique features. It is led by a well-established national party which has less than one-third of the seats in Parliament. The coalition includes a large number of parties from all over India, each of which has a relatively small number of members in Parliament and which have very little ideological affinity with each other. Each of these parties has only five to twenty-five members in the Lok Sabha which has a total membership of 543. The combined strength of all the coalition partners is, however, not sufficient for the government to command a majority in the House. The survival of the government depends on the outside support of another coalition by the Left parties, which have a combined strength of about sixty members (or 11 per cent of the House). The Left parties have promised their continued support to the ruling coalition while, from time to time, reaffirming their strong opposition to the policy orientation of the coalition in power.

As a result of internal differences among the coalition partners, domestic politics has become fluid and uncertain. Any party with a handful of members (say, less than 5 per cent of the total membership of the House) can stall even a unanimous Cabinet decision because of regional or other considerations. This was visibly demonstrated in July 2006 when the government was forced to cancel all decisions on disinvestments in public enterprises because of the opposition of one coalition partner. If this becomes an unavoidable feature of coalition politics in the long run, it would have substantially adverse consequences for the working of India's democracy. The following comments of a well-known academic writer echo a widely shared view:

> We seem to be moving beyond policy incoherence towards a much more alarming phenomenon that can be described as policy paralysis. Policy initiatives seem to be emanating from individual ministries rather than from the council of ministers, with different ministries often signalling different messages . . . It is perhaps time to ask whether a common enemy is a robust enough basis for the formation of coalition governments, or whether policy coherence needs to be more firmly consolidated as the cornerstone of coalition governance. If there is a lack of consensus on policy initiatives, the unending process of mutual spiking and checkmating cannot but result in policy paralysis. In that situation, governance is willy-nilly reduced to little more than the routine business of government, which can arguably be managed by the bureaucracy. But is that a desirable scenario for responsive and democratic governance?[2]

It is possible that the above fears are exaggerated. In view of India's intrinsic strengths, it is also likely that the economy will continue to grow and vital national interests will be fully protected. However, from the

long-term point of view, and in considering the need
for political reforms, what happens in the next year or
two during the life of a particular coalition is not
really all that relevant. What is important is to
recognize that in the foreseeable future, India is likely
to be ruled by a multi-party coalition of one type or
another. In the light of our own experience as well as
that of other countries, it is also likely that most
multi-party coalitions will have disparate ideologies
and programmes that are not shared by all the coalition
partners. Unless some new rules are put in place, the
governments formed by such coalitions may not have
much authority or credibility. In such situations, as
and when they arise, it is not difficult to visualize the
threat to the country's economic prospects and other
vital national interests.

Looking ahead, the important political challenge
now is to consider ways of making such coalitions
more effective in their functioning and less amenable
to pressures by small parties with a handful of members
in Parliament. In this connection, it is pertinent to
note that the emergence of multi-party coalitions,
formed with the participation of a large number of
small parties as the normal pattern of government,
was not foreseen when the original Constitution was
adopted. It is interesting that the present situation
regarding the possibility of the 'destabilization' of a
ruling multi-party coalition by a small party is in
some ways similar to the situation witnessed in several
states of India in the 1960s and 1970s when
governments with thin majorities were destabilized by
the defection of individual members from one party to

another. In order to prevent such defections, the 52nd Amendment adopted in 1985 called for the disqualification of a member from the legislature if he decided to give up membership of the political party to which he belonged. The 52nd Amendment was further amended in 2003 (91st Amendment) to make the disqualification provision even more stringent. Under the 91st Amendment, until the disqualified member once again gets re-elected to the legislature, such a person is not permitted to hold a public office as a minister or any other remunerative post during the remaining term of the existing legislature. In principle, the threat of destabilization of a coalition government by a small party, or for that matter by a few independent members, is not very different in its implications for political stability than that posed by the defection of one or more members from a particular party. This fact needs to be taken into account in determining the role of small parties in a coalition.

At present, while defence of the national boundaries and administration of the country's armed forces is entirely the responsibility of the Central government, the responsibility for the maintenance of internal law and order is that of the states. The Central government has control over multiple vigilance and intelligence agencies which, as and when necessary, provide information to the states about any perceived security threats in the areas controlled by them. Unfortunately, several states in India are witnessing a substantial erosion in their capacity to enforce law and order and to take appropriate action in response to intelligence information on security threats. Nearly one-fourth to one-third of all Indian districts are now believed to be under the influence of Naxalite organizations. This fact has been officially recognized, and serious concern about this development has been expressed at the highest levels of the government.

The reasons for the weakening of the law and order machinery in different states are varied, but one common feature is the extensive political interference in the police administration. The priority areas for police action are decided by ministers in power, and can vary from vigilance over 'dance bars' to provision of security to their preferred constituencies. Frequent transfers of top-ranking officials in the police administration are common. In some states, senior security personnel have been transferred more than once during the course of one year. Chiefs of police administration and other senior officers who take effective action to punish criminals are more likely to be transferred than rewarded. Thus, a sample poll taken by a national media organization has revealed some shocking statistics. According to this poll, conducted in June 2006, as many as 80 per cent of the respondents believed that corruption was widely prevalent in the police administration in their states. Even a larger number (84 per cent) were of the view that the police was open to political interference. In view of political pressure, the police was unable to stop legal violations and was inclined to tamper with or manipulate evidence, and indulge in other malpractices.[3]

In view of the fact that the nature and organizational structure of terrorism in India has changed over time, it is essential to evolve a different strategy to tackle the internal security problems. The division of political powers between the Centre and the states for supervisory responsibility over internal security and the intelligence agencies has to be redefined. This responsibility has to be centralized rather than diffused over a large number of states with different parties in power and frequent elections at different points of time over the five-year electoral cycle. Across different states, there is at present no effective and coordinated machinery for tackling terrorist threats from externally controlled organizations that have a global reach. The maintenance of normal law and order may continue to be the responsibility of state governments, but prevention of terrorist threats and serial bomb blasts of the type that occurred in Mumbai in July 2006 and earlier (including the attack on Parliament in December 2001), should be the responsibility of the Central government. A paramilitary apolitical organization along the same lines as the defence services with a well-defined internal security objective may need to be set up. This may require a change in the present distribution of powers between the Centre and the states through appropriate Constitutional amendments. Redistribution of powers on security matters between Centre and states has to be combined with a much greater devolution of powers to the states in economic and financial areas.

There is no doubt that India's economy is currently on a new growth path. Part of the reason for the resurgence of confidence in India's future is the process of economic reforms initiated in 1991. However, there is another important reason why there has been such a dramatic shift in India's economic outlook. The basic reason, which is sometimes overlooked, is that the sources of comparative advantage of nations are vastly different today than they were fifty or even twenty years ago (see Jalan 2001).[4] There are very few developing countries that are as well placed as India to take advantage of the phenomenal changes that have occurred in production technologies, international trade, capital movement and the deployment of skilled manpower. As a result, India today has the knowledge and skills to produce and process a wide variety of products and services at competitive costs.

The benefits of a favourable change in India's comparative advantage are already reflected in a sustained high rate of growth and improvement in its balance of payments. At the same time, income disparities in India between the poor and the not-so-poor, and between town and country, seem to be widening. It is a sobering thought that despite high growth and rising foreign exchange reserves, India continues to have the largest number of poor in the world, one of the lowest ranks in the global human development index, the highest rank in the corruption perception index, and a high degree of environmental pollution and deforestation. Public infrastructure, particularly in rural areas, where the bulk of the people live, is by all accounts abysmal. The trend rate of growth of agriculture, which provides a livelihood to 60 per cent of our population, has also been well below expectations. The share of India's agriculture in national income is now about 20 per cent. The organized sector of the economy has grown, but employment has not increased proportionately.

An important reason for the continuing poverty and growing disparity, despite a higher rate of growth of national income and greater export competitiveness, is what can be best described as the growing 'public–private' dichotomy in our economic life. It is a striking fact that economic renewal and positive growth impulses are now occurring largely outside the public sector, at the levels of private corporations, autonomous institutions and individuals at the top of their professions in India and abroad, and developmental work by non-government organizations. In the government or the public sector, on the other hand, we see a marked deterioration at all levels, not only in terms of output, profits, and public savings, but also in the provision of vital public services in the fields of education, health, water, and transport. The decay in the country's administrative and public delivery systems has affected the poor the most. They are critically dependent on the availability of public services and essential infrastructure, particularly in rural areas where 700 million or more Indians live.

As pointed out in my book, *The Future of India*, the country is now facing a crisis of governance.[5] By any criterion, the administrative system has become largely non-functional and unresponsive to the economic and social priorities of the country. Since Independence, the size of the government machinery has increased phenomenally, the number of ministries and departments has multiplied, and more and more programmes to provide relief and services to the poor have been launched in each of the ten Five-Year Plans. Some of the programmes have no doubt helped in reducing the worst forms of poverty and preventing famines. However, as is well known, because of administrative apathy, neglect, and diversion of resources to other purposes (including corruption), the overall results in eradicating poverty have so far been well below expectations.

Among the important political factors which, in my view, have contributed to accentuating the rich–poor divide and dualism in India's economy during a period of high growth are the following:

• Over the last five decades, the role of ministers in the governance of the country has increased and their accountability has decreased substantially. In response to the urgent need to reduce poverty, various ministries have been quick to announce ambitious programmes and annual as well as five-year targets for the benefit of the poor. However, no minister, or ministry, or the government as a whole has been held responsible or accountable for actual performance. Reports have been written, issues have been debated, and various policy and procedural violations have been highlighted by vigilance and other agencies from time to time. However, there has hardly been any effective response or 'action taken' at the political level to improve the situation except periodic declarations to banish poverty and help the common man.

- There has been an increasing politicization of the bureaucracy, and exercise of discretion by ministers, at all levels of the administrative hierarchy. Efficiency in the delivery of public services has been the main casualty.

- With multiple agencies and government departments generally working at cross purposes, the differences in views and policy approaches have been sent to higher and higher political levels for resolution. This has resulted in the proliferation of permanent and ad hoc Cabinet committees and groups of ministers, which meet from time to time and from case to case. Until these committees are able to take the necessary decisions, the administrative system comes to a standstill. With frequent elections and short tenures of ministers with different party affiliations, the decision-making process has become highly time-consuming and complex.

In the light of the above analysis, there is no doubt in my mind that we, as the people, must take stock of recent developments in the political, economic and security landscape of our country and take measures to further strengthen the functioning of our political system. We cannot, and must not, sit back on our laurels and bask in the glory of past achievements and the universal praise for India's emergence as an economic power of the twenty-first century. Unless we take resolute and urgent action, India may not be able to realize its full potential as has been the case with promises to remove poverty in each of the successive ten Five-Year Plans since 1951.

Let me now turn to a brief overview of the main theme of the subsequent chapters of this book.

Democracy, Growth and Distribution

The first chapter on 'Rewards and Discontents of Democracy' is an attempt to examine some of the analytical issues on the impact of political democracy on growth and poverty alleviation which have been extensively discussed in the development literature. In all democracies, there is a wide appreciation of the multiple freedoms that such a system confers on all its citizens. Political parties, whether they are in government or in Opposition and whether they are large or small, have the same rights. They also have equal access to the media and other channels of communication with the people, including the right to strike and promote or disrupt the normal processes of business in legislatures and elsewhere.

The impact of democracy on growth and poverty is an important political issue in all poor developing societies. In many countries in Africa, Asia and Latin America, the need to accelerate the pace of industrialization and growth provided a ready alibi for the imposition of dictatorial forms of government after independence from colonial rule. Some of them did well, but many of them stagnated. In response to internal popular pressures as well as international opinion, several countries have now opted for democratic forms of government. However, some of them continue to stagnate or face periodic external crises.

In view of past experience as well as the inability of several democracies to show decent rates of growth and/or alleviate poverty, a widely shared view among economic experts and political leaders is that while a democratic form of government is certainly politically preferable, it does impose some economic costs which have to be accepted as being unavoidable. In India also, the failure of successive governments to fully implement various anti-poverty programmes or improve productivity of public investment in infrastructure is often attributed to its vibrant democracy.

Fortunately, on this whole issue of the relationship between democracy and growth with equity, the statistical results of extensive cross-country experience in more than 100 developing countries are now available. The details of the research findings, and their analytical underpinning, are given in Chapter 1. The main conclusion emerging from the research is that the hypothesis that democracy necessarily leads to weaker growth is simply not tenable. There are as many cases of successes among democratic countries over different periods, as there are cases of failures. The economic outcomes are not related to the type of government a country has, but what a government does when it is in office. In fact, an important benefit of an open society is that if wrong policies are followed, a correction or reversal of these policies is easier. In closed and authoritarian societies, on the other hand, governments are more inclined to persist with wrong policies over longer periods.

Based on the findings of historical and statistical research, the most interesting question that emerges is not whether democracies can deliver satisfactory economic outcomes (in addition to political freedom), but why some democracies do so much better than others. The answer to this question is also relatively straightforward. The actual outcomes of policies are likely to depend on the quality of leadership and accountability of elected governments for their performance.

Against this background, the last section of Chapter 1 briefly examines the Indian experience on growth and poverty alleviation under a democratic political system. In some ways, India's own development experience over the past six decades confirms the above findings of research. Under periodically elected democratic governments, India showed impressive results in terms of growth and industrialization in the 1950s and early 1960s, followed by stagnation and persistent economic crises over a long period—upto the beginning of the 1980s. Since then, there has been a resurgence in growth rates, which has gathered further momentum at the beginning of the twenty-first century. However, notwithstanding high growth rates, a major failure in the past two decades has been in the pace of poverty alleviation and provision of minimum public services to the poor.

The reasons for governmental failure in the delivery of services are multiple, but a major reason is the lack of political accountability for administrative performance. The chapter ends with an examination of some recent political developments, which may further compound the problems and lead to increasing discontent with the working of India's democracy.

The Political Pyramid

In his classic book *Power*, published in 1938, Bertrand Russell examined the sources and uses of power by leaders in different types of private and public organizations, including government. The main point made by him was that, irrespective of the nature of the organization or the form of government, the preservation and expansion of power is likely to be the primary objective of those who inherit, usurp or are appointed to positions of power. Thus, according to Russell, even in democracies with free and periodic elections, 'individuals and organizations which are intended to have only certain well-defined executive functions are likely, if unchecked, to acquire a very undesirable independent power.'[6]

In view of the large electoral population and vital role of government in the economy, the politics of power has certain special characteristics in India. These are examined in Chapter 2. As in other federal democracies, the organizational structure of political power in India is 'pyramidal'. However, what distinguishes the Indian case from other federations is that the size of the electorate increases exponentially as a candidate moves higher up the ladder, while the number of political constituencies and available offices tend to shrink. In the jargon of economics, the mismatch between supply and demand for political offices increases sharply at higher levels, leading to an increase in the 'scarcity value' of such offices. While entry is relatively free and the number of persons elected to political offices is large at the bottom of the political pyramid (i.e. the Gram Panchayats), access to politics at higher levels (i.e. state legislatures and the Union Parliament) is highly restricted.

An important consequence of the high scarcity value of political offices at state or Central levels is the emergence of leaders who enjoy a 'monopoly' in the use and benefits of power. This explains the virtual disappearance of inner-party democracy from the Indian political scene. Aspiring and successful political leaders are inclined to set up their own regional or sub-national parties, which are in a position to win a few seats in legislatures or Parliament with the help of other parties in pre-electoral alliances. The Lok Sabha elections in 2004, for example, was contested by as many as fifty-five parties, with only two parties winning more than 10 per cent (but less than one-third) of the seats in the House on their own account. Another consequence of the high value attached to scarce political offices, and the 'demand' by parties for persons with organizational clout and money to contest elections, is the entry into politics of persons with a history of criminal offences and other legal violations. All Cabinets at the state and Central levels (with perhaps one or two exceptions) have a fair number of such persons in charge of sensitive ministries. In recent years, with the emergence of coalition governments, induction of persons with dubious backgrounds into political offices has become more acceptable and is considered unavoidable in the context of 'compulsions of coalition politics'.

As one moves up the political pyramid, the 'scope' of power available to leaders also increases sharply (in addition to the increase in the scarcity value of power). Unlike other well-established democracies, ministers and other political leaders in India enjoy enormous commercial and economic powers at the state and Central levels. At the Centre, the entire governance machinery of the country, a predominant proportion of fiscal powers, control over large public sector undertakings in crucial sectors (such as banks, insurance, petroleum and food distribution), and allocation of huge public funds for investments (in sectors such as power, roads, ports and aviation) are at the disposal of political leaders in office.

In India, control over public enterprises and the ability to launch new projects are important sources of commercial power. In addition to employing a large number of persons, public enterprises also account for a substantial proportion of the national output in industry and services. The production and distribution of goods and services involve issuing a vast number of contracts, appointment of dealers (such as allocation of petroleum pumps), fixing prices, and purchase of machines and materials. Along with the power to influence public sector decisions in these areas, ministers and other political dignitaries enjoy considerable free media publicity at the expense of public enterprises. India is unique in this respect as there is no other mature democracy in the world where newspapers and electronic media in different languages are full of advertisements issued by public enterprises, with photographs of ministers and other party leaders.

As elaborated in Chapter 2, the discretion available to ministers in the exercise of commercial and other statutory powers has led to substantial diversion and misuse of public funds. It is the primary cause of over-centralization, procedural bottlenecks and high cost of providing public services, particularly to the poor. There is an urgent need to reduce the vast scope of discretionary powers available to politicians in office, and thereby reduce the scarcity value of such offices. Certain measures to achieve these objectives, without in any way compromising with the legitimate responsibility of political leaders for determining the economic and other national priorities, are considered in the last chapter.

The Burden of Corruption

Chapter 3 deals with the widening spread of corruption in India and its high costs to society. Since the prevalence of corruption has become all-pervasive and everyone is aware of it, not much needs to be said on this subject in this introductory portion. Let me only emphasize three points, which may be of interest to the general reader in considering the need for political reforms in the functioning of India's Parliamentary democracy.

Hardly a day passes when the subject of '*Garibi Hatao*' (Remove Poverty) does not figure in speeches by political leaders in all parts of the country. This issue also figures prominently in debates in Parliament and state legislatures when they are in session. New programmes for achieving this objective are announced from time to time, particularly after a new government comes into office. However, an important finding of cross-country empirical research on the persistence of poverty in many low-income countries, which seldom figures in political discourses, is the widespread corruption in the delivery of public services. It has been found that government expenditures are often inflated, supply of food and health services are diverted, and wasteful projects are taken up for implementation in the name of poverty alleviation. A related finding is that the adverse economic effects of corruption are more pronounced on small enterprises, poorer regions and employment. Contrary to popular perception, the costs of corruption to society as a whole are disproportionately high, a major part of these costs is borne by the poor, and the benefits of corruption, which flow to the few, far exceed its costs. It, therefore, follows that the objective of poverty alleviation cannot be achieved without a frontal attack on corruption and elimination of the causes which give rise to it. This is the first point.

The second point, emerging from India's experience, is that part of the reason for the attractiveness of politics as a career of choice by persons with criminal records is the enormous judicial delay in deciding such cases. The investigative and prosecution machinery is under direct control of departments of the government. There is a natural reluctance to speed up investigations and the prosecution of persons who are leaders of political parties and/or members of the Cabinet. Thus, it has been said—with some justification—that in India, 'a person would rather be in politics than in jail'. According to a statistical survey of elections to the Lok Sabha in 2004, it was found that out of 3,182 candidates surveyed, as many as 518 candidates, cutting across all political parties, had criminal antecedents. Out of these 518 candidates, as many as 115 were elected to the Lok Sabha (which has 543 seats in all). It is no wonder that physical scuffles and assaults among some members on the floor of state Assemblies, and even Parliament, is not an uncommon sight when tempers rise because of charges of corruption and wrong-doing by leaders of one political party or another.

It is gratifying that there are still a fairly large number of persons of integrity, vision and social commitment in India's politics. A number of young and qualified persons are also gaining entry into state legislatures and Parliament. At the same time, it has to be recognized—however painful it may be for the average citizens to do so—that the systemic relationship between politics and corruption is increasingly becoming 'circular' because of the high cost of fighting elections. In recent years, elections at state as well as Central levels have also become more frequent than was the case earlier. The size of the electorate and the number of party candidates have also increased. Surveys of expenditure by candidates during national elections show that actual expenditure by a winner in the Lok Sabha elections was at least six times higher than the permissible limit fixed by the Election Commission for a candidate. This additional expenditure was generally incurred by political parties and other supporters, which does not come under the purview of the Commission's expenditure ceiling. In order to raise large funds to fight elections at frequent intervals, recourse to extra-legal sources of political contributions is now widely accepted as being unavoidable.

In addition to other measures to reduce the scope of corruption associated with political power and reduce legal delays, it is also imperative to provide for at least partial state funding for election expenditure. An equitable and workable formula for doing so, without imposing undue burdens on state or Union budgets, is discussed in a later chapter of the book.

The Role of Parliament

In some ways, Chapter 4, on the diminishing role of Parliament, is the 'core' of this book, and provides the main rationale for political reforms for India to be able to realize its full economic potential and face the emerging challenges to its security.

There has been a fundamental change in the role of Parliament since the emergence of multi-party coalitions as a regular form of government in India. The Parliament is still supreme. In order to remain in office, a government must enjoy the support of a majority of members in the Lok Sabha. However, what has changed in recent years is that the majority of members, which support the government, belong to a large number of different parties, inside and outside the ruling coalition. The leading party in the coalition, and some small parties inside it, may have a common ideology and a common programme. The survival of government, however, crucially depends on the support of one or more parties which have different ideologies and different support bases. Several of them, while united at the Centre, are deeply divided at the regional and state levels.

The tenure of office of a coalition government, which takes office after national elections, is naturally uncertain. The general expectation, at least in the initial years, is that the new government will not last its full term of five years. Since 1989, the country has undergone as many as six general elections and a majority of incoming governments had brief tenures ranging from a few days to about one year. The dependence of a new government on the support of parties, which are otherwise opposed to it, has had several unintended consequences for the functioning of Parliament and other vital pillars of India's democracy.

Parliament now has multiple centres of power (in addition to the party leading the government, and the party leading the opposition). An important consequence of the emergence of multiple centres of power is that what the Parliament does or does not do depends on 'behind the scene' agreements among different sets of party leaders within and outside government. As long as the government has the backing of leaders with majority support, it is supreme and it can get Parliament to do what it wishes.

Chapter 4 provides a detailed account of the happenings in Parliament during the period 18–22 March 2006 during the Budget Session. These five days saw the culmination of a process of decline in the role of Parliament, the supreme organ of the State. It should be mentioned that what occurred during those days had also happened in earlier years—but not in combination nor over such a short period. The decisions taken by the government between 18 March and 22 March, and approved by Parliament, included a drastic revision in the business of the two Houses, the passage of the Budget and the Finance Bill by 'voice votes' without discussion, the suspension of the procedure for consideration of the Budget by Standing Committees, followed by the sudden adjournment of Parliament *sine die*. What was equally surprising was that, after its adjournment, it was decided to reconvene the Parliament again after a few days, more or less as per the earlier schedule. The Standing Committees were also asked to consider the Budget after the Parliament had already approved it!

During those five days, the Parliament also approved the controversial 'Office of Profit' Bill, which was later returned by the President to Parliament for reconsideration. It will be recalled that the Parliament did reconsider this Bill in its next session, but it was pleased to approve it in its original form and send it back to the President for his assent.

The above is a brief account. The details provided in Chapter 4 about the proceedings of Parliament over five days are worth reading in order to fully appreciate the changing role of Parliament vis-a-vis the executive. I should emphasize that the purpose of highlighting the wider implications of multi-party coalitions in the functioning of Parliament, and other areas of governance is not to undermine the legitimacy of coalitions in a democracy. Coalitions are expressions of the will of the people in a diverse polity with multiple, and often irreconcilable, party interests. As in several other countries, coalitions are also—from time to time—unavoidable in a parliamentary system of government or for that matter in a presidential system with a separate legislature.

At the same time, it has to be recognized that if disparate multi-party coalitions have become a regular feature of our governance system, then certain changes in parliamentary procedures, the role of small parties, and systems for enforcing accountability of the executive for its decisions are also essential. This is particularly so in a country which is characterized by widespread poverty, disparity and deprivation among its people. It is possible that in other more developed and advanced democratic states, unstable and self-serving governments may not cause as much damage to the larger public interest as may happen in a developing and predominantly rural society.

Separation of Powers

In parliamentary democracies, patterned on the British model, the Council of Ministers is supposed to be collectively responsible to Parliament for the performance of the government. All policy decisions of the government, irrespective of the individual ministries which initiate and implement them, are expected to have been approved by the Cabinet or its committees, and represent a consensus among all members of the Cabinet. A corollary of the principle of collective responsibility is that no individual minister can be held formally accountable for the failure of a ministry to implement a decision or a programme announced by the government. In other words, no minister is *individually* responsible for actions and decisions taken on behalf of the government.

Another long-standing principle for the conduct of business in parliamentary democracies is that the day-to-day executive functions are carried out by a permanent civil service, which is selected through an open and competitive procedure. The civil service reports to politically appointed ministers and the Cabinet, but members of the civil service are expected to be apolitical in their functioning. Under civil service rules, they are not permitted to join any political party, and are obliged to render advice without taking any party-political interests into account. An independent and apolitical civil service is supposed to ensure that, while politics is the responsibility of ministers, the day-to-day business of the nation is carried out in accordance with approved policy without fear or favour of particular interests or sections of the people.

Unfortunately, as explained in Chapter 5, over time, the principle of collective responsibility of the Cabinet and that of an apolitical civil service have undergone some important changes in the coalition era with low life expectancy of governments. Important ministerial berths are assigned on the basis of the size and strengths of leaders of different parties, and individual ministers are practically free to do what they wish. Cabinet approval may be taken, where mandatory. Often, important policy changes with long-term implications (such as, changes in curricula of national educational institutions) are announced by individual ministers without Cabinet approval. Subsequently, in the case of a change in government, the incoming minister is free to reverse the earlier decision or modify it.

With increasing frequency of appointments and transfers of civil servants on party-political grounds, the politicization of the bureaucracy has also gathered momentum. According to one study, cited in Chapter 5, in the large state of Uttar Pradesh (where, for a while, there was an agreement for a six-monthly rotation of heads of government between two parties in a coalition), transfers of officers, including those from the IAS (the Indian Administrative Service) and IPS (the Indian Police Service), ran at an average of seven per day. Under the second head of government, who took office after the expiry of six months, such transfers rose to sixteen per day! Over half the corps of IAS officers, at the top of the official hierarchy, was transferred within twelve months of their posting. It is not surprising that civil servants in several states are now inclined to play safe and promote the interests of their political masters. The costs to society, particularly the poor, of the above developments have been substantial. New programmes may be announced by ministers, but they do not take individual responsibility for non-performance or diversion of resources. Civil servants may be appointed to sensitive positions on political grounds, and even if they are not, party labels are likely to be assigned to them by competing civil servants and others.

In order to improve the functioning of the government, and provide minimum services to the people, it is now essential to hold ministers individually accountable for the performance of their ministries in implementing programmes announced by them. The government can continue to be collectively responsible to Parliament for its survival in office and proving its majority on legislative and budgetary matters. Similarly, some administrative reforms are required urgently to make the civil service more accountable and responsible.

The last section of Chapter 5 deals with the issue of separation of powers between judicial and executive branches. There is unanimity among experts as well as members of legislatures and the judiciary that the principle of separation of powers among different organs of the state is an essential feature of India's Constitution, and that it should remain sacrosanct. However, the question of where precisely the boundary of separate powers of the legislature and the executive vis-a-vis the judiciary should be drawn has become a matter of some controversy. The legislative and executive branches consider themselves supreme for taking decisions on legislative changes (for example, in respect of reservation quotas for OBCs, i.e. Other Backward Classes; exemption of specific offices in different states from the purview of 'Office of Profit'; or disqualification of members of Parliament/ legislatures on ethical grounds). The judiciary, on the other hand, considers itself Constitutionally responsible for deciding on the legal validity or otherwise of any specific policy or other measures approved by Parliament/legislatures.

There are valid arguments on both sides. After examining these, for reasons explained in Chapter 5, my conclusion is that, on balance, the country is better off with the judiciary as an additional checkpoint on legality of actions taken by the legislature and the executive. The people should have the unfettered right to appeal to the judiciary on the Constitutional validity of legislative decisions taken at the behest of the executive.

An Agenda for Political Reforms

The ten-point programme of political reforms, proposed in the last chapter of the book, is an attempt to resolve some of the emerging problems in the functioning of India's parliamentary democracy. The proposed programme is relatively modest in scope. It is also consistent with the parliamentary form of government and the present electoral system.

The two most important objectives of the proposed agenda for reforms are to increase the life expectancy of coalitions at birth, and to improve the conduct of business in Parliament. In order to achieve the first objective it is proposed that the anti-defection laws should also be made applicable to members of all small parties (below a prescribed threshold) and independent members of a legislature who opt to join a coalition government. At present, this law is applicable only to members who decide to defect from their parties. This law is not applicable if a particular party, however small, decides to defect from a coalition government. Thus, for example, if five members of a larger political party (with, say, a total of twenty members) decide to defect then they have to seek re-election. They are also not entitled to hold any public office during the remaining term of the Parliament or legislatures until they are re-elected. If, however, the same five members were members of a small five-member party and the party decides to defect from the coalition government, then the present anti-defection law does not apply. Small parties are free to join a coalition, then leave it, and join another coalition of parties in order to destabilize the existing coalition government.

There is no justifiable reason why members of a small party should be put in a more favourable position than any other group of defecting members. In fact, it can be argued that the present exception of a small number of members, who form a separate party, from anti-defection laws provides a built-in incentive for fragmentation of a large party into smaller parties at the time of elections. This adds to the expectation that a coalition government will not survive for long.

In order to strengthen the role of Parliament and reduce its subservience to the executive in the conduct of its business, it is essential to adopt some rules which cannot be altered or suspended arbitrarily at the behest of the government. In order to avoid the recurrence of events which took place during the five days of 18–22 March 2006 (see above), it may be specifically provided that the established rules of procedure in the two Houses cannot be suspended or amended after a session of Parliament has been formally convened, except in a national Emergency declared by the government with the approval of the President. It should also be made compulsory for the Budget and the Finance Bill to be passed only after consideration by the concerned Standing Committees of Parliament. In case sufficient time is not available because of special circumstances (such as election schedules), then only a 'vote-on-account' should be approved. Similarly, all Bills and other legislative business of the government should be adopted only after a division and counting of votes of members, and not by 'voice votes'. In case, because of disruptions, Parliament is unable to conduct its legislative business, in a democracy, it is much better for the public to be aware of it rather than carry the impression that Parliament is functioning normally and as per established procedures.

Another important objective of the proposed agenda for political reforms is to reduce the scarcity value of political offices at higher levels by reducing the 'scope' of powers available to ministers and increasing the transparency in the exercise of such powers (see Chapter 2). The Right to Information Act, adopted in 2005, is likely to contribute substantially to making the decision-making processes of government transparent and subject to public scrutiny. Further simplification of the administrative procedure and a drastic reduction in the number of agencies, at different levels, which are involved in granting sanctions, would also contribute to this process.

The ministerial discretion in taking case-by-case decisions in order to implement an announced programme or policy should be eliminated altogether, and replaced by an 'arm's length' and transparent administrative procedure. In order to reduce the scope of ministerial powers in economic and financial areas, the direct role of government in the management of commercial enterprises deserves to be substantially reduced. On the other hand, the government's direct role in ensuring the availability of public goods (such as roads and water) and essential services (such as health and education) to the people should be strengthened. Ministries should set annual targets in these areas and ministers should be held individually responsible for actual performance in relation to announced targets in Parliament.

Another area where immediate action is necessary is that of lowering the bar on political corruption. In recent years the tolerance for political corruption at high levels of government, Parliament and legislatures has become common (see Chapter 3). A lid has to be put on the tolerance levels of corruption, and persons who have already been 'charge-sheeted' for corruption and similar criminal offences should not be permitted to take the oath of office and function as ministers until they have been cleared by the courts. A special procedure may be set up to expedite the disposal of pending court cases against persons who are proposed to be appointed as ministers. A broad-based reform of the entire legal and judicial system in order to reduce delays in the disposal of cases and eliminate the huge backlog of pendencies is, of course, another priority area for reforms.

Much has been said and written about the need to provide state funding for electoral expenses of political parties in order to curb political corruption. Some large democracies, like the US, have taken some steps in this direction. However, in India, it has not been possible to reach a consensus on this issue. Two frequently voiced objections are: (a) the likely fiscal burden, and (b) the difficulty of working out an equitable distribution formula for the allocation of State funds among a few large parties and numerous small parties which contest elections. So far as the fiscal burden is concerned, it is likely to be relatively small in relation to the total size of Central and state budgets. In any case, if considered necessary, it is possible to reduce the additional fiscal burden on this account by reducing some other types of political expenditure (for example, allocations to Members of Parliament for local area development). Similarly, it is feasible to devise a workable and equitable formula for the distribution of State funds, which takes into account the size of parties as well as essential requirements of small parties. One such scheme is suggested in Chapter 6.

As mentioned at the beginning, these and other suggestions in the proposed agenda for political reforms are relatively modest and consistent with the parliamentary form of government. They also do not break any new ground. They are in conformity with recommendations made by several high level official commissions and committees as well as amendments to the Constitution approved by Parliament in the past (for example, in respect of defection of elected members from political parties). Still, I have no illusion that the necessary changes to make the present system more accountable would be easy to accept or implement because of conflicts of interests among different sections of the political spectrum. Much would depend on the willingness of political parties to modify their short-term interests and on the collective response of the civil society in favour of measures to further strengthen the democratic process.

References

1. Inter-American Development Bank (2006), *The Politics of Policies: Economic and Social Progress in Latin America*, Harvard University, USA.

2. N.G. Jayal (2006), 'Has the UPA Government Lost Control?', Debate, *Economic Times*, New Delhi, 11 July 2006.

3. *Times of India*, New Delhi, 25 July 2006 ('Cops in the Dock', p. 2).

4. Bimal Jalan (2001), *India's Economy in the Twenty-first Century: A New Beginning or a False Dawn*, The Eighteenth C.D. Deshmukh Memorial Lecture, India International Centre, New Delhi, 15 January 2001. (Reprinted in Bimal Jalan, *India's Economy in a New Millennium: Selected Essays*, Delhi: UBS Publishers Distributors, 2002).

5. Bimal Jalan (2005), *The Future of India: Politics, Economics and Governance*, New Delhi: Viking, 2005 (Penguin edition, 2006).

6. B. Russell (1938), *Power*, London: George Allen & Unwin Ltd. Reprinted as Routledge Classics 2004, Routledge, UK, p. 232.

ONE

The Rewards and Discontents of Democracy

The functioning of India's democracy has been a subject of debate and critical examination by several eminent authors in recent years. There is universal praise for India's success in strengthening its electoral processes, and protecting the fundamental democratic rights of its citizens. In the context of political developments in several newly independent developing countries as well as other countries across the world, this is generally regarded as an amazing achievement of which India can be justifiably proud. At the same time, the persistence of illiteracy, poverty and gross inequality among large sections of the people is a puzzle that has been difficult to resolve.

In this chapter, I propose to examine some of the theoretical and analytical issues that have been extensively discussed in the development literature about the impact of political democracy on economic growth and poverty alleviation. There is a view that part of the reason for India's relatively low rate of growth over the past five decades, as contrasted with that of China, was due to the democratic form of government. A related view is that even if growth were higher (as was indeed the case in India after 1980), it need not necessarily have led to a more equitable distribution of income. It has been observed that democracies are institutionally less capable of delivering a faster rate of poverty alleviation because of their preference for providing 'visible' and direct subsidies to the poor. Such direct subsidies are often misappropriated by better-off sections of the population.

My general conclusion on the above analytical issues, which are considered in some detail in the next two sections, is that there is no inherent contradiction between having a democratic form of government and the ability of that government to adopt policies designed to generate high growth and alleviate poverty within a reasonable period of time. At the same time, for the reasons discussed in the last section of this chapter, I also believe that for India's democracy to be able to deliver better economic results, some reforms in the existing institutional structure of India's political system are essential, particularly in the light of more recent developments. There is also an urgent need for citizens, their elected representatives, and other organizations to exercise greater responsibility for the functioning of our democracy and for holding the government accountable for its performance in relation to declared objectives.

Growth and Democracy

An important issue, which has been discussed extensively in the development literature, is that of the relationship between growth and democracy. In this connection, a frequently cited example of the negative relationship between the two is that of a democratic India which, despite extensive controls over the economy and adopting centralized planning after Independence in 1947, registered one of the lowest rates of growth in the developing world until the early 1980s. China, on the other hand, was able to achieve a persistently high rate of growth over the same period. This was at least partly due to its ability to achieve a high rate of capital accumulation with rapid industrialization under an authoritarian political system. China did not have to go through periodic elections and changes of government with the attendant waste of time, resources and effective governance. A similar example is that of East Asian countries, particularly Korea, Singapore and Taiwan. The East Asian countries also achieved persistently high rates of growth over a long period under a political system that was different from that of China, but which was still highly authoritarian, conceding only limited degrees of freedom to the people.

The contrast between the poor growth record of India (and that of some other democratic countries) and the much more impressive records of China and East Asia in the 1960s and 1970s is certainly striking. However, what is equally relevant is the fact that there are a large number of dictatorial regimes in Africa, Asia, and Latin America that have experienced equally low—if not lower—rates of growth as democratic regimes, including India. The example of a country like Zimbabwe, which has experienced not a rise but actually a sharp decline in incomes under an authoritarian regime, is a testimony to this fact. Indeed, the number of dictatorial regimes that have experienced economic deprivation and disasters at different points in their history is perhaps larger than in democratic countries.

In view of the widespread interest in the impact of different political systems on economic outcomes, the results of a comprehensive statistical examination of the cross-country historical experience are also now available. The conclusion of this research, based on the experiences of more than a hundred developing countries over several decades, is that the hypothesis that democracy *necessarily* leads to weaker growth is simply not tenable (Przeworski, 1995[1]; Barro, 1996[2]; and Przeworski and others 2000[3]). According to a recent study, 'the lists of miracles and disasters are populated almost exclusively by dictatorships . . . The [economic] tigers may be dictatorships, but [all] dictatorships are no tigers'. (Przeworski, A. and others, 2000, p. 178).

The reason why some countries do better than others does not depend on the type of government that a country has, but rather on what the government actually does. It is self-evident that the policies and circumstances that led to economic success under some authoritarian regimes such as those in Southeast Asia in the 1970s and 1980s are not intrinsically related to the nature of their regimes. They are eminently replicable in democratic countries, as India's experience in the 1990s shows. Constructive policies for higher growth (for example, openness to competition, literacy, health, industrial liberalization, and export orientation) can be pursued as effectively in a democracy as in a non-democracy, if the government so desires. Similarly, China's policies of openness to foreign direct investments, high savings, and high exports can also be pursued by a democracy. Thus, India's policies aimed at achieving external viability and a strong balance of payments position in the 1990s have been as, if not more, successful as the policies adopted by East Asian countries before and after the crisis of 1997. India was also able to achieve a higher rate of growth despite the pace of reforms being slower. East Asian countries are also freer and more democratic in the post-crisis period than they were before. The change in the nature of their regime has not hurt their growth or external viability.

Authoritarian political systems, however, have one advantage over democracies that deserves to be recognized. This concerns the implementation of programmes and policies. Given equal opportunities and the right policies, it is likely that an authoritarian government that wishes to do so, will be able to accelerate its growth more quickly and achieve higher rates of productivity than a democratic government. It is likely to be less encumbered by the power of special interests. It, therefore, needs to waste less time and resources in reconciling political differences among various sections or regions. Given a choice, a democratic system with a lower rate of growth is still preferable to a dictatorial system with a higher rate of growth. However, it is important to ensure that the process of conflict resolution through democratic bargaining does not become an end in itself at the cost of public at large.

India's development experience in the 1960s and 1970s provides an interesting example of how the power of special interests in a democracy can effectively reduce growth rates below a country's potential. This can happen in two ways. First, the benefits of growth, development policies and public investments can be diverted to powerful interest groups, such as large surplus farmers (through subsidized credit and high procurement prices), industrialists (through monopolistic licensing, protective tariffs and subsidized inputs), organized workers (through job protection and high wages), civil servants (through their control over public delivery systems and public enterprises), and politicians (through their control over government decision-making processes). Second, the delivery of government benefits to special groups, with scarce resources, can lead to the emergence of a large number of middlemen across the political spectrum. Further, as elections become more expensive and more frequent, political corruption is regarded as an unavoidable feature of the democratic electoral process.

Fortunately, for India, even though special interests, and their coalitions, still remain politically powerful, the freeing and opening up of the economy has reduced their hold over it, particularly in the 1990s. After a long period of stagnation during the period 1966–80, the economy began to emerge slowly from the darkness. Despite cyclical ups and downs, for nearly two decades after 1981, India's annual growth rate was close to 6 per cent (as compared to 3 per cent in the earlier period). The growth rate was close to 8 per cent in 2004–05 and 2005–06, and there is considerable optimism that by 2020 or 2025, India will emerge as one of the three most important global economies. As I will argue later, whether the current optimism about India's long-term prospects is actually realized would very much depend on the working of India's political institutions.

In considering the relationship between democracy and growth, it is important to recognize that an important benefit of democratic functioning and free speech is that, if wrong policies are followed, a correction of these policies is easier and unavoidable in view of public pressure and open discussion. Correcting unviable policies can be delayed, but cannot be avoided altogether. Similarly, it becomes difficult and untenable for a democratically elected government to ignore the suffering of the people due to droughts or floods, which are quite common in countries like India and where a large proportion of the population is dependent on agriculture. The role of democracy in preventing famines has also received considerable attention in this context. Thus, it is noteworthy that India has not had a real famine since Independence despite endemic undernourishment and malnutrition. China, on the other hand, had the largest famine in recorded history during 1958–61, when wrong public policies led to disastrous results. The authoritarian government was able to continue with its policies despite widespread starvation for as long as three years. As a result, nearly 30 million people died because of lack of food. This could not have occurred in a country with a free press. The benefits of democracy are clearly apparent both in terms of what it has been able to achieve, and even more important, in terms of what it has been able to prevent.

To sum up the discussion so far, if the right economic policies are followed, a democracy is as capable of yielding high rates of growth as an authoritarian regime. The statistical evidence on this point is also unequivocal and supports this view. Non-democracies and dictatorial systems can implement government directives more effectively, but by the same token they can also make irreversible mistakes that can cause immense distress to the people and undermine their growth potential. Conflict resolution among different interests in a society is an important aspect of democratic functioning, and it may no doubt impose a resource cost in terms of growth and efficiency. Even so, the verdict of history on the preferences of the people is clear and unambiguous. Democracy and its multiple freedoms are valuable to the people for their own sake and have to be protected and nurtured, whatsoever the short-term economic costs. It is the responsibility of democratic governments to ensure that such costs, if any, are minimized, and that the power of special interests in diverting national resources is curbed in the interest of the public at large.

Votes and Equity

Periodic elections to seek the people's mandate for the government to continue in office (or otherwise) are truly a triumph for India's democratic traditions. In the national elections held in May 2004, as many as 675 million people were entitled to vote. More than 400 million persons exercised their franchise. This was the largest democratic election ever held in the history of the world. What is also remarkable about Indian elections is that a preponderant proportion of the voters is from poor rural areas. In urban areas also, there is evidence that the poor tend to vote much more than the middle and upper classes (Yadav 2000).[4] For all Indians, and for others interested in democratic elections, it is exhilarating to see all candidates, including powerful ministers and party leaders, campaigning from time to time for the people's vote with the utmost humility and respect.

Yet the fact remains that along with the largest electorate in the world, India also has the largest number of persons living below the poverty line. Even the most conservative estimates released by government agencies show that as many as 300 million Indians are below the poverty line, and do not earn enough to provide even the minimum intake of food and nutrition. Conditions prevailing in India's urban slums and rural areas are also among the worst in the world.

The peaceful co-existence of the power available to the poor to elect their representatives and their continuing poverty is a puzzle that has baffled political scientists, ideologues, and development economists. Why do citizens continue to vote into office persons who, after the elections, become prisoners of special interests and divert public resources to meet their own or their party's interests at the expense of the poor?

Why is it that people continue to tolerate the widespread failure of public delivery systems in health, sanitation, literacy, and basic civic facilities? The answers to these questions are not easy, and this is not the place to go into them in any detail (see, for example, [Varshney 1995][5] and [Weiner 2001][6]). A part of the answer lies in the division of the poor along ethnic, caste, and religious lines across the country, high incidence of illiteracy, particularly female illiteracy among the poor, and acceptance of non-performance as an unavoidable feature of India's political system.

The paradox of the persistence of poverty along with the power to vote raises two analytical issues concerning the relationship between growth and equity. The first is whether there is an inherent conflict between high growth and the equitable distribution of the fruits of that growth. The second issue is whether democracies are institutionally less capable of delivering a faster rate of poverty alleviation because of their preference for providing visible subsidies to the poor (e.g. subsidized food or fuel which does not really reach the poor) as compared with the pursuit of the 'right' economic policies. The latter are designed to maximize returns and higher productivity in the use of national resources (which are likely to benefit the poor indirectly over a longer term). Let us briefly discuss these two issues.

On the relationship between growth and poverty alleviation, as it happens, the global experience is that countries and regions that have registered high and sustained rates of growth over a reasonable period of time are also the ones that have achieved the best results in reducing poverty and improving the health and nutrition of their people. In some cases, the progress in reducing poverty or improving the level of human development indicators has no doubt been much greater than would seem warranted by their rates of growth, as has happened in Kerala and Sri Lanka. There are also cases where high growth has been combined with a worsening of the poverty ratio (e.g. Brazil in the 1970s), or where high per capita incomes have not resulted in adequate progress in education and other social services (e.g. some oil-rich countries). However, such cases are not many and they have their own special reasons. It is also becoming evident that some countries like Sri Lanka, which despite low growth had made commendable progress in poverty alleviation in the past, are now finding it difficult to sustain the process. Per capita expenditures on anti-poverty programmes have declined because of fiscal stringency.

It is obvious that poverty alleviation in a low-income country with poor basic amenities and poor availability of essential public services (such as primary education, water, power and transport) is feasible only if the government has the financial capacity to create the necessary infrastructure for the provision of such services for the poor. It is also likely that the higher the rate of growth of the economy, the higher will be the growth of government revenues and its capacity to finance social expenditure. Whether the government actually does so or not is naturally a matter of public policy. However, a low growth rate is not pro-poor. Nor does it help the debate on social or public policies. It is legitimate to ask for more government expenditure and more government intervention in favour of the poor or for more pro-employment growth policies. But it is fallacious to argue that the government can be more pro-poor in a stagnant or low-growth economy for any length of time.

On the question of 'direct' and 'indirect' approaches to poverty alleviation, there are two conflicting viewpoints. One view is that democratically elected governments are more inclined towards the direct approach because of their higher visibility. However, the direct approach is not as effective as some (though not all) indirect growth-based methods, nor is it fiscally sustainable (Varshney 2005)[7]. The opposite view is that the so-called 'trickle-down effect' of high growth on poverty alleviation is largely illusory. In any case, the positive effects may take much too long to occur. Therefore, the direct approach of providing employment through public works, and social entitlements in the form of food and public services, is likely to be more effective and quicker in providing relief to the poor.

On closer examination, it seems to me that the distinction between so-called direct and indirect approaches to poverty alleviation is untenable. It stands to reason that in developing countries with a large proportion of the population below the poverty line, faster alleviation of poverty is not feasible unless the government provides access to low-cost facilities to the poor for education, health, and other basic amenities. At the same time, it is also true that the government's ability to provide employment through public works, and social entitlements in the form of food and public services is critically dependent on its ability to finance social entitlements, which in turn depends on the growth of revenue and income in the society. The greater the growth of the economy, the greater will be the capacity of the government to finance social expenditure.

India's past experience also supports this view. For a quarter of a century, after the Second Plan was launched in 1956, India had a highly centralized government—a directed planning system with the avowed aim of eliminating poverty and achieving full literacy by 1980–81. The actual achievement was nowhere near this objective. India continued to remain mired in high levels of poverty, illiteracy, and infant mortality. The root of the failure during this period lay in low efficiency of resource use. This was the reason for the low growth of national income despite a substantial increase in the rate of national savings and investment. After 1964, with higher fiscal deficits, India also began to face a severe resource crunch along with periodic balance-of-payments crises.

After 1980–81, growth rate in per capita incomes has been much higher—more than twice the level achieved in the previous thirty years. However, the rate of poverty alleviation still broadly remains at about the same level as earlier because of inadequate allocation and diversion of public resources. The answer to the puzzle of India's higher growth rate after 1980–81 combined with persistent poverty lies in what can perhaps be best described as the growing 'public–private' dichotomy in our economic life. It is a striking fact of our present situation that economic renewal and positive growth impulses are occurring largely outside the public sector. In the government or the public sector, on the other hand, we see a marked deterioration at all levels—not only in terms of output, profits, and public savings, but also in the provision of vital public services in the fields of education, health, water, and transport. These two elements— fiscal deterioration and the inability to provide essential services—are, of course, intimately connected. In India, most of the public resources are now dissipated in the payment of salaries to staff and interest on debt, with little or no resources available for the expansion of public or publicly supported services in vital sectors.

To combine votes with equity, we need both— that is, high growth as well as direct government action—to provide access to basic public facilities and food security for all.

The Price of Liberty

It is clear that so far India's democracy has not been able to deliver adequate economic benefits and essential public services to a substantial proportion of its people, who otherwise have the right to vote and elect their government from time to time. Although India was able to accelerate its overall growth performance after 1980, this did not result in commensurate improvement in the pace of poverty alleviation or better access of the poor to public services. A further disquieting development in recent years has been the erosion in the accountability of the government to Parliament for its performance in the context of coalition politics and the general public acceptance of the view that 'politics will be what it will be'. It is felt that if the government is unresponsive to the people's requirements, so be it; the people at least have the benefit of democracy and its multiple freedoms. The economy is anyway growing faster and the people, including the poor, are free to do what they wish. Sooner or later, it is hoped that everybody will be better off.

I do not share the above views about the irrelevance of politics in shaping India's economic future. In this section, I propose to draw attention to some recent political developments that are matters of serious public concern. My purpose in drawing attention to these developments is simply that, unless some countervailing action is taken, the working of our democracy as envisaged in the Preamble to our Constitution, and the freedoms associated with it, can not be taken for granted for all time to come.

Let me cite two examples, one historical and one contemporary, to underline the importance of this point. The American War of Independence occurred in the 1770s and gave birth to a federal and democratic United States of America. The United States also adopted a written constitution in 1787, which has not only survived for more than two centuries but has also become a model of sorts for all democracies in identifying certain unalienable and fundamental rights and principles of governance for their own

constitutions. The same federal and democratic USA
(which was an inspiring example during India's
freedom struggle in the first half of the twentieth
century) underwent a civil war—between the Southern
states and the Northern states in the 1860s, i.e. nearly
ninety years after its War of Independence. If that
well-established democracy was saved from division
or disintegration, it was largely because of the
unflinching determination of the federal government
to preserve the Union under the leadership of Abraham
Lincoln. The history of the United States is a useful
reminder that, although we can be justifiably proud of
our own democratic history of sixty years since
Independence (with only one interruption during the
period of the Emergency from 1975 to 1977), the
preservation of democracy in a diverse union of states
and peoples cannot be taken for granted.

This leads me to my second example, which
relates to the working of democracy in the state of
Uttar Pradesh in India. Uttar Pradesh has the largest
number of seats in the Indian Parliament. It has a
population of 175 million (which is substantially
larger than the combined population of two of the
oldest European democracies, the United Kingdom
and France). In this important state, no party has
received a clear majority since 1991. Due to internal
squabbles and personality clashes among leaders of
coalition partners, the chair of chief minister has
virtually become a revolving one. The state has had
ten changes in the office of the chief minister since
1991. Some chief ministers have taken office for a few
months, then relinquished it, and then come back

again for a few months. For a couple of years after 1997, there was an agreement between two large alliance partners, with opposite ideologies, that each party would rule the state in turn for six months each. Even this understanding could not lead to a stable government, and soon there was a fresh realignment of parties. In view of these developments, a leading newspaper observed in a recent editorial that governance and politics in Uttar Pradesh 'has been heading steadily towards anarchy . . . It is obvious that money is playing a big role in the current flurry of activity. In any case, ideology has ceased to be an issue in UP politics. Money and muscle power injected into the polity by a new breed of politicians, have reduced statecraft to management of caste, religious, and gang loyalties. This muddy mélange of criminals, dalals and career politicians, their roles overlapping, is a threat to democracy.'[8]

The unease about the working of our political system is now widely shared not only by the media but also by independent political observers. The deterioration of political norms in Uttar Pradesh has reached a point where, in February 2006, a Cabinet minister in the state belonging to a religious minority announced a large monetary reward for the murder of a Danish cartoonist who had printed some highly offensive and sacrilegious cartoons in his newspaper in Denmark. The public announcement of a reward for murder is against all canons of jurisprudence and established laws in India, irrespective of the seriousness of the offence or the crime committed by the offender. Yet the minister continued to remain in office even though his pronouncements had the effect of inciting political passions and rioting. The riots were followed by strong communal tension in a state that was historically known for its communal harmony.

Problems of a similar nature, although of a lesser magnitude, have recently occurred in several other states. Among them mention may be made of the controversies surrounding the formation of governments in the states of Bihar, Jharkhand and Goa after state elections in early 2004 (some of these events are covered in Chapter 5). In some other states, alliances were formed by erstwhile bitterly opposed political parties in search of more electoral seats or greater accommodation in power-sharing arrangements (for example, in Karnataka and Tamil Nadu in April–May 2006). Taken separately, such developments can be considered minor aberrations affecting particular states without any repercussions at the national level. However, taken together, recent developments in electoral politics at the state level are matters of serious concern. To quote a recent editorial from a business newspaper:

> At one level, India is a modern economy emerging from the shadows. At another, it is regressing into political medievalism, where the operative word is not law but power. This medievalism is characterized by the emergence of a feudal order whose chief feature is the emergence of what can only be called the mansabdari system of Mughal India. It's the size of the tribute and the number of horsemen (read MPs or MLAs) that determine political worth. If you have enough horsemen, you are de facto above the law, or indeed become the law.[9]

If the growing trends towards political opportunism and partisan action by Constitutional authorities spreads further, there is no guarantee over the long run that the democratic values at the national level will continue to be safe. In case political alliances at the Centre also become unstable and short-lived, political opportunism of the type witnessed in some states may also occur at the federal level without any safety valves in place. At present, the Centre has the power to impose President's rule in a state in the event of prolonged instability. At the federal level, no such recourse is available as the Union Cabinet is supreme and the President can act only on its advice. Some countervailing action is, therefore, necessary to curb the worst kind of political opportunism, which has the potential of undermining the very foundations of a stable, prosperous, and democratic India.

As a counter to the above view, it may be argued that concerns about the survival of India's democracy are as old as the birth of the republic. It will be recalled that at the time of Independence, there was worldwide scepticism about the future of India as a united democratic republic. India had then an untried government combined with widespread communal violence and social disorder. In view of its immense regional, linguistic, and religious diversity, it was apprehended that India would soon break up, or at least go back to an authoritarian regime of some kind. And yet, because of its inherent strengths and pre-Independence history of inclusiveness of various conflicting forces, democracy in India has not only survived but has also become 'deep and strong' (Desai

2005).[10] India has also emerged as one of the fastest-growing developing countries, with strong social, cultural, and economic bonds across its regions.

From a historical perspective, the above viewpoint is certainly correct. However, it misses out on some of the more recent, and still incipient, developments which pose a threat, not to the mere survival, but to the working of Indian democracy in the interest of the people at large rather than a handful of their leaders (Khilnani 1998).[11] The deterioration in the working of India's democratic system (leaving aside the aberration of the imposition of the Emergency during 1975–77) is relatively recent and has not yet become the order of the day in all the states or at the Centre. But, as pointed out above, the contagion is spreading. It is, therefore, necessary to take countervailing action to impose some checks and balances in the actual functioning of India's democracy in the light of more recent developments. Among these developments, which deserve to be taken cognizance of, are the following:

- Coalitions that last less than five years in office are likely to become the norm at the Centre and in the states rather than the exception. By any standards, India's founding fathers gave the country a great Constitution after its independence from British rule. However, it is doubtful whether, against the background of the predominance of a single party (the Indian National Congress) and its inclusive nature during the Independence struggle, the fathers of our Constitution visualized the possibility that the country will be ruled, on a regular basis, by a coalition of several parties (as has been the case since 1989). In the light of developments during the past sixteen or seventeen years, there is a need to set some 'norms' for the behaviour and conduct of parties in a coalition government.

- Legislatures, which are supposed to represent the will of the people, have become the handmaiden of the executive and the party or parties temporarily in power. In the coalition era at the Centre and in several states, small parties with 5 or 10 per cent of the seats in Parliament can enjoy enormous balancing power as the price of their support to the government from inside or outside. Many of them represent regional, religious, caste or sectional interests. They are, however, under complete control of their leaders, who are free to switch sides, nominate members to the Cabinet (or, for that matter to the Rajya Sabha, the Upper House of Parliament), and decide who will contest elections in preferred constituencies.

- In principle, the executive is accountable to the legislature, as enjoined by the Constitution. However, the accountability is largely *pro forma* as long as the government enjoys the support of the majority of the members in the coalition. Any law, however sectional or partisan in its intent, including the budget of the government, can be passed without debate.

The judiciary is independent but over-burdened with pending cases, some of them for over a quarter of a century. For an ordinary citizen, India has plenty of laws but little justice.

- It may be argued that in all parliamentary systems, the decisions of the executive are paramount as long as it has a majority. However, the difference between our system and other mature systems is that, in India, the executive has substantial economic and financial powers (many of them highly discretionary) than is the case in other parliamentary democracies.

- It is no secret that politics is generally regarded as the most lucrative business in the country, with few checks and balances (Subramaniam 2004).[12] It has become an attractive occupation for persons with a criminal record. In addition to power, a political position provides strong protection against conviction or punishment. During elections, every major party has its fair share of candidates with a string of pending court cases against them. A number of them also get elected, and some of them become members of the ruling cabinet, wielding wide powers directly (or indirectly through their Cabinet colleagues) over investigating agencies, the police and even the lower rungs of the judiciary. Political corruption has always existed, but what has changed in recent years is its high-profile coverage in the media along with public acceptability that it is an unavoidable feature of Indian life.

- The relationship between the political masters and the civil service bureaucracy (including public sector managers) has also tilted heavily in favour of the former because of their unlimited powers to transfer, appoint, and provide post-retirement sinecures (Kumar 2004).[13] The economy has been liberalized, but ministries at the Centre and in the states continue to have a substantial hold over economic activity through various means (for example, allocation of land, power, taxation, government contracts, and subsidies of various kinds). The power of ministers to take even the most minor administrative decisions on behalf of the government is based on the premise that the political executive is accountable to the people through their representatives in Parliament or in state legislatures. This assumption, as mentioned above, does not have much validity.

- The difference between being in power as a minister in the government and being an ordinary member of the legislature, in terms of perquisites, staff, and official displays of pomposity (for example, through the provision of security guards, red lights and other paraphernalia), has increased substantially. There is an enormous sense of deprivation among those who are no longer ministers or those whose parties have lost power after having enjoyed it for some time. This has led to an unseemly scramble for power and offices by politicians at different levels, and has increased the power of party leaders enormously. As a result, the process of inner-party democracy has been adversely affected. The leaders of different parties are ready and willing to switch sides without regard to the programmes or ideologies of contesting coalitions. To reduce the sense of deprivation on loss of office (and vice versa), it is necessary to eliminate the colonial pomp and splendour attached to ministerial offices.

The above is by no means an exhaustive list of developments that need to be addressed for strengthening the functioning of democracy in India. There are many more areas that require attention. These, along with some additional suggestions for the reform of politics, will be taken up in the later chapters.

A democratically elected government remains the best option for India even if the present deficiencies are not addressed in the short term. Even in those states where poor administration and bad governance are the norm, an elected government is a better option over the long term than a non-elected one. India's experience with the Emergency (1975–77) and the widespread abuse of power by persons in authority provide adequate support for this view. The people's verdict in 1977 was unequivocal and the Congress party, which was in power during the Emergency, was voted out unceremoniously for the first time after Independence. Obviously, people preferred their rights of freedom to all the other economic benefits promised by the then government, and rightly so.

At the same time, while people certainly prefer their freedoms and the right to elect their governments, there is also a strong feeling of discomfort and disenchantment among them about the functioning of India's democratic system. They are wary of the politicians whom they elect, and distrust the gargantuan civil service apparatus that has ostensibly been set up for their benefit. It should be possible to make the democratic system work much better and more effectively for the common person, provided we are determined to do so.

Let me conclude with an observation by Amartya Sen, who has made an enormous contribution to our understanding of the advantages of democracy and the obligation of citizens to derive maximum benefit through constant vigilance. 'Democracy does not serve as an automatic remedy of ailments as quinine works to remedy malaria. The opportunity it opens up has to be positively grabbed in order to achieve the desired effect.' (Sen 1999)[14] The achievements of democracy depend not only on the rules and procedures that are adopted and safeguarded, but also on the way that opportunities are used by the government in response to popular pressure. Democratic institutions are no doubt important in the functioning of a democracy. However, they should not be viewed as merely mechanical devices for development. Their successful use is dependent on societal value and priorities, and on effective public participation in ensuring the accountability of the governance structure.

References

1. A. Przeworski (1995), *Sustainable Democracy*, Cambridge: Cambridge University Press.

2. R.J. Barro (1996), *Getting It Right: Markets and Choices in a Free Society*, Cambridge, Mass.: MIT Press.

3. A. Przeworski, M.E. Alvarez, J.A. Cheibuk and F. Limongi (2000), *Democracy and Development: Political Institutions and Well-Being in the World, 1950–1990*, Cambridge: Cambridge University Press.

4. Y. Yadav (2000), 'Understanding the Second Democratic Upsurge', in Frankel, F. et al. (ed.), *Transforming India*, New Delhi: Oxford University Press.

5. A. Varshney (1995), *Democracy, Development and the Countryside*, Cambridge: Cambridge University Press.

6. M. Weiner (2001), 'The Struggle for Equality: Caste in Indian Politics', in A. Kohli (ed.), *The Success of India's Democracy*, Cambridge: Cambridge University Press.

7. A. Varshney (2005), 'Democracy and Poverty' in D. Narayan (ed.), *Measuring Empowerment*, Washington DC: World Bank Publications.

8. *Times of India*, New Delhi, 4 March 2006, p. 32.

9. *Business Standard*, New Delhi, 22 February 2006, p. 13.

10. M. Desai (2005), 'Why is India a Democracy?' in M. Desai and A. Ahsan (eds.), *Divided by Democracy*, New Delhi: Roli Books, p. 73.

11. S. Khilnani (1998), *The Idea of India*, London: Penguin.

12. T.S.R. Subramaniam (2004), 'All the Netaji's Men', *Indian Express*, 17 September 2004.

13. A. Kumar (2004), 'Chasing a Will o' the Wisp?', *Indian Express*, 25 September 2004.

14. A.K. Sen (1999), *Development as Freedom*, New York: Alfred A. Knopf, p. 155.

TWO

The Politics of Power

The previous chapter highlighted some of the rewards and discontents of democracy in India. Democracy is alive and well, but there have been some recent developments in its institutional framework, which have considerably reduced its effectiveness in serving the people. Democracy, like any other form of government, confers enormous powers on those who are elected or appointed to offices of the State. The great advantage of a democratic form of government, as compared with more authoritarian regimes, is the accountability of elected representatives to the people, particularly at the time of periodic elections. Unfortunately, in India, while elections are free and fair, they have not been able to 'get men of power to live *for* the public rather than *off* the public'. This was not always the case, and even today there are many honourable exceptions among politicians who have given up their successful professional careers in order to serve the people. However, as a rule, there is a common and widely shared perception that politics is now a profession of choice for those who enjoy the benefits of power and the various immunities that it confers.

All parties, old and new, nominate some persons with a history of criminal offences or other legal violations to contest elections. Governments in all states (with perhaps one or two exceptions) have Cabinets that include a fair number of such persons in charge of sensitive ministries. In recent years, with the emergence of coalition governments, this is also the case at the Centre. A common defence of this practice is that persons with criminal records have been elected 'by the people'. Therefore, in a government 'of the people', they cannot be denied their just rewards. Interestingly, at the time of appointment or entry into professions, this argument is not applicable to any other public servant or to members of any other profession. An interesting consequence of the special position accorded to criminals in political life is that the 'demand' for entry into politics by those whose cases are pending in judicial courts at different levels has increased substantially. The 'supply' of offices or constituencies to meet this rising demand has, however, not kept pace.

The organizational structure of political power is 'pyramidal' in shape. It is wide at the base or the grassroots where the number of persons elected to political offices, such as gram panchayats, is large in number and entry is relatively free. However, the number of such offices shrinks drastically at the district, state or Union levels. The size of the electorate increases exponentially as one moves higher up the ladder, while the number of political constituencies and offices become fewer. The higher the level of an office, the pyramidal structure of political power increases the mismatch between supply and demand for that office and increases its scarcity value.

This phenomenon partly explains why at higher political levels, entry into politics has become more and more restrictive. Access to politics at the higher levels (with some honourable exceptions) is now available only to persons with sufficient 'clout', in terms of family connections, money, ethnic and caste loyalty, and/or coercive power. Competitive politics has also made electoral politics expensive, which has further reduced its accessibility to the average person who lacks adequate means, power, and command over a community's resources.

Another consequence of the high value attached to scarce political power is the emergence of leaders who enjoy a 'monopoly' in the use of power. This explains the virtual disappearance of inner-party democracy from the Indian political scene. Most parties, again with a few exceptions, have leaders who alone (or with the help of some trusted aides) decide who will fight elections, who will join the Cabinet, and who will get nominated to various political and government offices. In case there is a threat to the power of a leader from another aspiring member of the same party, that member is likely to be expelled or declared *persona non grata*. Alternatively, if that aspiring member has adequate political strength and following, the original party is likely to be split. Parties may also be split from time to time for other reasons, such as joining a coalition in power or accepting the inducements offered by an aspirant with money or clout. As a result, the number of parties vigorously contesting elections shows a secular increase over time, with most parties winning only a few seats. The Lok Sabha elections in 2004 were contested by as many as fifty-five national and regional parties, with only two parties winning more than 10 per cent of the seats in the House on their own account. Almost all parties, including the two largest parties and some other parties, had entered into pre-electoral alliances with other parties, but each party continued to be guided by its own leader before and after the elections.

As one moves up the political pyramid, the 'scope' of power available to leaders also increases, further enhancing the scarcity value of power and demand for such offices at higher levels. At the village level, the principal responsibilities entrusted to political representatives are relatively few. These include identification of beneficiaries under poverty alleviation and employment generation schemes, distribution of subsidized agricultural inputs, local infrastructure projects and miscellaneous welfare schemes (such as old-age assistance, disaster relief, and housing programmes for the poor). However, they have very little budgetary or financial powers to raise resources, and the bulk of fiscal resources for poverty alleviation programmes are allocated by the Central and state governments. Village-level panchayats also generally have no role in the delivery of education and health services to residents. The operation of primary or secondary schools and public health centres continues to remain under the control of state government officials and their political masters.

The scope of powers available to political leaders increases enormously at the state and Central levels. At the state level, in addition to a hundred or more Centrally sponsored and state poverty alleviation and other schemes, there are a large number of infrastructure projects under management or construction. Another important source of financial power is the state co-operative banking structure with its district co-operative and primary co-operative societies, which are fully or largely under the control of political representatives. In addition, there are numerous public sector commercial or service organizations, which have been set up by state governments and are directly under the control of political leaders in administrative ministries. State governments also have practically unlimited powers to establish new agencies and public sector organizations, with separate budgets and separate management structures. The appointments to managerial positions in these organizations are under the direct control of individual ministers or Cabinet committees, and are subject to change when a new government comes to power.

At the Centre, of course, the entire governance machinery of the country, the predominant proportion of fiscal powers (including exclusive jurisdiction over custom tariffs and corporate taxation), the large public sector undertakings in important sectors of the economy (such as banks, insurance, petroleum, food procurement and food distribution), and control over allocation of national resources (including investment in crucial sectors, such as power, roads, aviation, and ports) are under the control and direction of political leaders. All matters relating to defence and external affairs, including defence procurement, are the exclusive preserve of the Central government.

A recent development that has considerably increased the power of party leaders at the Centre, at the cost of state legislatures, is the amendment in the eligibility criteria of candidates for election to the Rajya Sabha (the so-called Council of States at the Centre). Earlier, only persons resident in a state were eligible for election by that state's legislature to the Rajya Sabha. As in respect of all other elections, these elections were also through a secret ballot, so that legislators could exercise their franchise freely. The residence criterion as well as the provision of secret voting has recently been withdrawn through legislative amendments to the applicable rules. The central party leaders are now empowered to nominate any person of their choice from anywhere in the country to represent a state in the Rajya Sabha. As the voting by legislators is open, and subject to a whip, the legislators have practically no choice in choosing their representatives. In principle, membership of the Rajya Sabha is now open to any person without any knowledge of the problems pertaining to, or having any connection with, the state that he or she is expected to represent in the Council of States. As the field is wide open and the number of seats is limited, after the recent amendments, the scarcity value of Rajya Sabha seats has also increased substantially.

At this point, the reader must be wondering: Why all this noise and fuss about political power? It is well-known that politicians, as representatives of the people, enjoy a great deal of power in all spheres of public life. This, after all, is the essence of democracy. The government is expected to work in the interest of the people, and it is their representatives who have to ensure that this is so. Unfortunately, this proposition which is entirely valid in theory, has become highly vitiated in practice, particularly in democracies where governments enjoy substantial power over the allocation of resources in the economy, including the savings of ordinary people and investments by the public and private sectors. This is true of India also, despite the economic reforms of the 1980s and 1990s. For example, individual ministers in different ministries are fully empowered to change tax concessions or tax rates (with the pro forma approval of Parliament and the Cabinet), or to change educational or urban development policy (with or without Cabinet approval). We will consider some of these issues in greater detail later. What is indisputable is that as the 'scope' of power available to political leaders and scarcity value of this power has increased, there is a growing disjuncture between the use of political power for promoting public interest as against sectional, party or private interests.

In recent years, the issue of private use of public power has also received considerable attention in the theoretical literature on institutional and development economics (for example, by Schleifer and Vishny [1998][2] and Dixit [2006][3]). Predation by the State or its agents (i.e. leaders in government) is believed to be the essence of the problem of continuing poverty in many countries, including democracies. Thus, according to Dixit, 'In conventional theory, when the government is the principal, its objective is assumed to be social welfare, and constraints include the need to raise some resource required for public expenditures. But when the government is predatory, its objective is to maximize its own take from the economy, and the constraints include lower bounds on the consumption or utility it must provide to workers to keep them alive, or perhaps to prevent them from staging a revolt against the government.' Fortunately, in India, although politicians enjoy enormous powers, there are also several checks and balances in the exercise of these powers, which has so far limited the extent of predatory action.

My purpose in drawing attention to the vast scope of political power, its rising scarcity value, and its pyramidal organizational structure is to highlight the need for political reforms in the future without compromising on socio-economic priorities. The enormous discretionary powers available to politicians at different levels of our society has had several unintended consequences, including diversion of fiscal resources for the benefit of the better-off sections of society at the expense of the poor, uneconomic selection of projects, increase in bureaucratic complexity, and criminalization of politics. These adverse economic, developmental and social effects of enormous political power, in an environment of fiscal stringency, judicial delays and administrative apathy, are not widely appreciated. Some of these adverse effects are discussed below.

I should clarify that in a large country like India, the situation varies a great deal from one state to another. Within the same state also, there are significant variations in the effective implementation of programmes and in the exercise of political power in the allocation of resources. Some states, under an enlightened leadership, do quite well from time to time, while others may remain mired in sloppy leadership and widespread diversionary practices. Similarly, as already mentioned, not all politicians are alike in their orientation. Several of them work selflessly to maximize the public good even under the most adverse circumstances. Subject to these caveats, I believe that what is said below is a fair description of the way that political power is exercised at different levels of our society for personal or sectional gains rather than for the common good.

Political Opportunism

Political opportunism is a euphemistic phrase, commonly used in the literature of behavioural economics to describe the bias among elected representatives at different levels to divert resources under a particular government programme to their own villages, constituencies, or states. Generally, such 'political opportunism' is also regarded as a legitimate exercise of power in furthering the interests of a particular group of constituents. Thus, it is quite common for the leaders of different parties, when in power, to ensure that disproportionate benefits under various government programmes flow to their own electoral constituencies. A strong vested interest also develops among residents to re-elect their leaders. Leaders of state parties also have the same preferences and derive the same benefits in terms of periodic re-elections. Interestingly, there is a tacit understanding among leaders of different political parties, whether they are in power or in the Opposition, that their constituencies and interests will receive preferential treatment in the allocation of governmental resources. With changes in coalitions and governments every few years, there is a mutuality of interest among political leaders in nurturing their constituencies, however antagonistic their political positions may be in public.

On the face of it, all of this sounds reasonable and acceptable. But the cost of such preferential treatment for society as a whole can be substantial in view of the scarcity of resources available under a particular programme. Thus, a particular constituency or area may get much higher benefits irrespective of the number of poor among its residents or the average level of income. It is a common experience that the number of beneficiaries under an employment generation or poverty alleviation programme is disproportionately high in the constituency or state of a leader or minister. A neighbouring state or district may be entitled to the same benefits, but is unlikely to get these even if it is poorer and more deficient in respect of the availability of public services. Another consequence is that political opportunism results in a substantial diversion of resources to those who are otherwise ineligible. Thus, for example, employment benefits and access to cheaper food (for BPL or

'Below Poverty Line' families) may flow to those who are already employed and whose incomes are well above the BPL level.

In India, one of the most remarkable political developments in the area of democratic decentralization was the passage of the 73rd Amendment to the Indian Constitution in 1993. As is well known, this Amendment created a new tier of local government which, by the year 2003, led to the constitution of as many as 2,35,000 new village governing institutions, i.e. gram panchayats, staffed by over two million elected representatives. This is probably the largest number of persons elected to serve as people's representatives in any democracy in the world. Further, as a remarkable experiment in affirmative action, the 73rd Amendment mandated that close to half of the elected positions be reserved for traditionally disadvantaged population groups (lower-caste groups and women). Although these village panchayats enjoy very limited financial powers, they have an overwhelming responsibility for beneficiary selection for government welfare programmes. The gram panchayats function under an elected leader, the 'pradhan', who has the main executive responsibility of identifying beneficiaries. The pradhan of a gram panchayat is accountable to the gram sabha, a body in which all villagers are entitled to participate. This again is perhaps one of the most impressive experiments in the field of direct democracy anywhere in the world.

The actual working of gram panchayats and gram sabhas, and the process of political selection and the quality of government resulting from it, have been subjects of extensive research (see, for example, the World Bank study [2005][4], and Besley, T., et al. [2005][5]). The overall conclusions of these studies are generally positive about the working of gram panchayats and their contribution towards improving the quality of grass-roots democracy in India. It has been found that when gram sabhas are held, the benefits are likely to be better targeted towards the poor and the disadvantaged. At the same time, it has been found that political opportunism by pradhans is also widespread. As a rule, the home villages of the pradhans tend to receive more high-spillover public goods than other villages of the gram panchayats (after accounting for factors such as village size). In order to maximize political opportunism and to take advantage of large-scale illiteracy in villages, pradhans are also reluctant to convene meetings of the gram sabhas on a regular basis.

With the expansion of corruption at different levels of the political pyramid, and public acceptance of it, corruption at the level of panchayats is also becoming more widespread. A most bizarre and obnoxious development, reported recently, is that of open public auctions in several villages of Tamil Nadu for the posts of panchayat presidents, vice-presidents, municipal and town ward members. As reported in newspapers, biddings for such posts were taking place in village squares or temple premises in districts (including Madurai, Krishnagiri and Vellore), with at least one post of panchayat president going for Rs 6 lakh.[6] The money raised through such illegal and unwarranted auctions is supposed to be used for purposes such as 'temple funds' or 'welfare funds'. There is little doubt that those who paid money to win panchayat positions would use their newly acquired powers to divert public resources to themselves.

While political opportunism is increasing at the level of the gram panchayat, according to field studies, the extent of such political opportunism is so far much less than it is at the state level. Part of the reason for this is the visibility of the pradhan, and his or her direct accountability to the gram sabha. Another related finding is that the higher the level of literacy and education in a village, the greater is the accountability of the pradhan to his or her constituents. In order to prevent the misuse of office and corruption among pradhans, some further safeguards may be introduced by legislation. Among such safeguards are: the obligation to convene meetings of gram sabhas at least once every month, public disclosure of all decisions made by pradhans, and strict enforcement of the Right to Information Act.

With the additional safeguards, an appropriate measure for improving the performance of anti-poverty and employment generation programmes should be to devolve the entire budgetary allocation to the gram panchayats without any direct involvement of state governments or Central government agencies. So far, however, the 73rd Amendment to the Constitution has only led to the creation of another tier in the distribution of resources at the local level. State government agencies and Central ministries are just as

involved in managing the programmes as they were
before the establishment of gram panchayats. Indeed,
in all the states as well as at the Centre, there are
separate Panchayati Raj ministries, and political leaders
at these levels and their officers continue to have
substantial supervisory and allocative powers in the
functioning of gram panchayats. According to media
reports, the Centre is also considering setting up a
whole new District Panchayat Administrative Service
(DPAS), which will further increase bureaucratic
complexity and reduce the political accountability of
pradhans to gram sabhas.

Fiscal Disempowerment

In India, the people's representatives either in the state
legislatures or in Parliament have practically no
effective role in matters of taxation or allocation of
expenditure under various government programmes.
There is certainly a pro forma role in the sense that
the budgets of governments have to be formally
approved by the legislature. However, in practice, all
the relevant decisions are made exclusively by a few
top leaders in the government, and are approved by
the legislature as desired by the executive, sometimes
without any discussion whatsoever. The Budget
Estimates, the Revised Estimates, the Final Accounts,
the Performance Budgets, the Outcome Budgets, and
the reports of the Comptroller General of India are
regularly presented or tabled in the legislature.
Sometimes, they are also discussed. But, so far, there
is no evidence that any person, any agency or any

ministry has been held accountable for any deviation in budgetary receipts or expenditure or any malpractices or failure to achieve promised outcomes or targets.

Over time, while the number of programmes of all kinds has increased phenomenally, fiscal resources for financing such programmes have become more stringent at the Centre as well as in all the states. Another common feature of budgets at different levels (including districts and gram panchayats) is that most of the budget allocation under different heads is spent on the salaries of government officials responsible for the execution, supervision, and monitoring of the various programmes. Capital expenditure for the improvement of infrastructure and/or revenue expenditure for providing monetary benefits or services to the people seldom exceeds 10 per cent of the budget allocations (except in a few programmes, which also suffer from substantial diversion of resources to unintended beneficiaries). In some states, the interest paid on accumulated state debt is virtually equal to the total revenue collected by the state, leaving very little for expenditure on any development programme.[7]

A good example of the substantial diversion of subsidies and budgetary resources to unintended beneficiaries under an important poverty alleviation programme is that of the Targeted Public Distribution System (TPDS). Under this programme, in order to provide food security, certain quantities of foodgrains are provided under the public distribution system (PDS) at highly subsidized prices to households with

incomes below the poverty line (BPL). The objectives
of these programmes are indeed laudable and are
supported by all sections across the political spectrum.
However, an evaluation study covering sixty districts
and 3,600 households undertaken by the Planning
Commission in 2005 has found widespread diversion
of grain from genuinely poor families to other
households.[8] Among the findings, the following are
particularly disturbing:

- During 2003–04, sixteen large states covered
  under the study were issued 14 million tonnes
  of food from the Central Pool for distribution
  to BPL families. Of this, less than 6 million
  tonnes (or only about 40 per cent) were
  delivered to the BPL families, and the rest
  never reached them.
- Thus, for every kilogram of food grain delivered
  to the poor, the Government of India had to
  issue 2.4 kg of subsidized grain.
- Out of an estimated budgetary consumer
  subsidy of Rs 7,250 crore for sixteen states in
  2003–04, as much as Rs 4,200 crore did not
  reach BPL households. Of this, nearly Rs 2,640
  crore of subsidy never reached any consumer,
  either below or above the poverty line, but
  was shared by the agencies in the supply
  chain.
- The government spent Rs 3.65 through
  budgetary food subsidies to transfer Re 1 to
  the poor.

There could not be a more serious indictment of
the government delivery system for the poor than the

above findings. The study has been discussed among the concerned ministries as well as in Parliament, but no solution has been found to the underlying causes of inefficiency and malpractices. Part of the problem in distribution arose from the simple fact that there were as many as four different prices of food grains from the same shop (varying from Rs 2 per kg to Rs 6.10 per kg) depending on the level of income of the buyer. Naturally, this led to the issuing of false BPL cards and substantial leakages in the distribution chain. Part of the answer to this problem could lie in the issuing of 'vouchers' equivalent to the implicit subsidy amount to BPL families and/or in drastically reducing the differentiation in issue prices in very poor districts where the bulk of the residents are BPL households. However, these proposals or other measures aimed at reducing leakages have not found acceptance at the political level, perhaps because of the persuasive powers of the unintended beneficiaries and the agencies in the distribution chain.

Political leaders and ministers have virtually unlimited powers to announce new schemes and programmes or to replace and re-designate old programmes, but they have no fiscal room available to implement these programmes because of the huge waste of resources on existing programmes. Interestingly, fiscal disempowerment has led to increasing bureaucratic complexity and higher salary expenditure, as procedures and checks to minimize budgetary outgoes on legitimate programme expenditure have multiplied! This is true in all spheres of government activity—from the highest levels of educational institutions to primary schools, from

nationally reputed research hospitals to basic health-
care centres in villages, from the transmission of
power in metropolitan cities to non-electrified areas,
and so on. According to an observer of the Indian
scene, who has also been involved in monitoring the
implementation of development schemes on behalf of
an international institution, despite the introduction
of ambitious and expensive government programmes
in almost every sector of human development since
Independence, over a quarter of India's population
languishes below the poverty line. A huge proportion
of those above it also remain vulnerable to slipping
back into poverty with a single shock, such as a
natural disaster or illness. According to him:

> A crucial impediment in India's march to
> development is the quality of its public expenditure.
> It is generally recognized that there is a very poor
> connect in India between the quantum of public
> money allocated and the accessibility and quality of
> services delivered. Money disbursed is often taken
> as a mark of money well spent; no matter that the
> allocated fund-flow often peters out leaving the
> problem unresolved, the school half-finished, the
> electric line half-laid, the road half-paved. (Carter
> 2006)[9]

The indifference of some state governments in
implementing welfare, employment or other anti-
poverty programmes after announcing them is so
great that, despite fiscal stringency, they sometimes
hold large cash balances with the Reserve Bank of
India. This happens because of the increase in the
mandatory transfer of the states' shares in Central
taxation as recommended by the Finance Commission

from time to time, increase in Plan grants, higher receipts from small savings, and advance aid disbursements by international donors. While ongoing projects remain unimplemented, higher budgetary transfers remain unspent pending the inauguration of new schemes, appointment of new staff, and payment of salaries, etc. This state of affairs, without accountability, is a direct consequence of the enormous budgetary powers enjoyed by political leaders in office. Ironically, these budgetary powers are conferred on them by most democratic constitutions on the ground that 'there should be no taxation without representation' and the belief that political leaders are the ones who alone are accountable to the people in deciding how budgetary resources should be spent. This noble principle is now honoured only in its breach.

Alternative methodologies and mechanisms for implementing decisions taken by political leaders at the policy level are entirely feasible and practical, provided there is adequate devolution of administrative powers at the lower levels. However, this has not been found politically acceptable. Indeed, as we shall see later, there is a consistent tendency to centralize decision-making powers in government ministries, even in respect of so-called autonomous organizations. This is an unavoidable consequence of the search for more power at higher levels in the political hierarchy.

Public Dis-savings

After Independence in 1947, as is well known, India adopted a highly controlled and Centrally directed strategy of development. While the reasons for adopting a State-dominated development strategy are understandable against the background of colonial rule, by the mid-1950s it had also become clear that the results of this strategy in generating self-reliant high growth were far below expectations. Thus, in as many as thirty out of the forty years between 1950 and 1990, India had balance-of-payments problems of varying intensity. Looking back, it is hard to believe that for as long as four decades after 1950, India's growth rate averaged less than 4 per cent per annum and that per capita income growth was less than 2 per cent per annum. This was during a period when the developing world, including sub-Saharan Africa and other least developed countries, showed a growth rate of 5.2 per cent per annum.

However, the most striking failure was not in terms of growth or even in terms of the precarious balance-of-payments situation. The most conspicuous development for which there is no alibi, and for which the responsibility lies squarely and indisputably with the deterioration in India's administrative system, is the erosion in public savings and the inability of the public sector to generate resources for investment or for the provision of public services.

It will be recalled that an important assumption in the choice of post-Independence development strategy was the generation of public savings, which could be used for higher and higher levels of investment. However, this did not happen, and the public sector, instead of being a generator of savings for the community's good, became a consumer of the community's savings. This reversal of roles had become evident by the early 1970s, and the process reached its culmination by the early 1980s. By then the government had begun to borrow not only to meet its own revenue expenditure, but also to finance public sector deficits and investments. During the period 1960–75, total public sector borrowings (including government borrowings) averaged 4.4 per cent of GDP. These increased to 6 per cent of GDP by 1980–81, and further to 9 per cent by 1989–90.

Thus, the public sector, which had a commanding presence in almost all industrial sectors of the economy, particularly heavy industry, gradually became a net drain on society as a whole. It is interesting to note that the Central government's total internal public debt reached a stupendous Rs 500,000 crore by the mid-1990s, and nearly one-third of it was accounted for by assets held in the public sector. Interest payments on public debt at that time amounted to nearly Rs 40,000 crore, which were financed by new net borrowings and which represented nearly 70 per cent of the Centre's fiscal deficit. In effect, one-third of the interest payments was on account of the government's past investment in the public sector. By the end of the 1990s, the Centre's internal debt had almost doubled to Rs 970,000 crore. This sharp increase was partly accounted for by the need to borrow larger and larger amounts to service the debt.

With the adoption of the Fiscal Responsibility and Management Act (FRMA), and a reduction in fiscal deficit, the overall situation in respect of public savings in 2003–04 and 2004–05 showed an improvement. As a proportion of GDP, after several years of negative savings, gross domestic savings in the public sector turned positive (to 1 per cent of GDP in 2003–04 and 2.2 per cent in 2004–05). There is still a vast gap— of more than 5 per cent of GDP—between savings and investment in the public sector. This gap is financed through market and other borrowings. Nevertheless, the recent positive development in reducing fiscal deficits is most welcome.

Against this background, an issue that deserves consideration is the reason for the political acceptance of dis-savings at the expense of the larger public interest. The answer is not far to seek. Control over the public sector and the expansion of government expenditure, at the cost of people's savings, is a source of considerable political power. All government expenditure, however costly to the society as a whole, benefits some individuals or sections of the people who are the beneficiaries of such expenditure. Since political leaders have the power to decide where to spend and which special groups to benefit, a higher level of government expenditure is always preferable to a cut in expenditure (see Olson [1965][10] and Becker [1983][11]). As pointed out in the vast literature on public choice, the 'coalitions of special interests' are strongly in favour of policies that redistribute national income and government expenditure in their direction rather than in adopting policies for growth or stable prices.

Another major source of power is the control over public sector enterprises. These enterprises provide considerable employment opportunities. They are typically over-staffed and pay higher than market wages, particularly at clerical levels with strong unions. Public enterprises are also dominant in a number of important sectors of the economy, including the financial sector, which has a large number of public sector banks and insurance companies with branches in all parts of India. The top management and the boards of directors are appointed by administrative ministries with the approval of the appointments committee of the Cabinet. There are selection boards for recommending names for consideration by the government for appointment as chairpersons, executive directors and board members. However, the final decision rests with the minister concerned and the Cabinet Committee.

There is nothing wrong with the above-mentioned procedure for selection and appointment as it seeks to combine seniority and professional competence with political acceptance in the choice of personnel at top levels of management. However, in recent years, with frequent changes in the ministers in charge of different ministries belonging to different parties, there has been a subtle change in the weights attached to the selection criteria. As appointments are subject to the discretion of the minister concerned, with little or no previous administrative experience in the ministry allotted to him or her, eligible contenders for the top offices (who also have short tenures before retirement) are more inclined to use political contacts to influence appointments in their favour. Control over public enterprises, particularly in the financial sector and in regions dominated by a few large manufacturing units, has become an important source of political power for leaders of parties represented in the government. There is a built-in incentive for setting up new public sector units or branches since their location and the selection of staff at these locations are also subject to political discretion.

In addition to employing a large number of persons, public sector enterprises are important providers of goods, transport and services, including telecommunications. The production and distribution of these goods and services involves issuing a vast number of contracts, appointment of dealers (such as allocation of petroleum pumps), and purchase of machines and materials. Decisions in all these areas, except large procurement contracts, are by and large in the exclusive jurisdiction of the management of public sector enterprises. Nevertheless, enterprising ministers and political leaders are in a position to exercise substantial 'invisible' influence in the use of these commercial powers by public enterprises because of discretion available to them in making appointments, granting extensions and effecting transfers of top executives. The exercise of such invisible powers need not necessarily lead to monetary corruption, but it confers substantial discretionary powers in the allocation of the nation's resources and in distributing other economic benefits.

Another advantage of control over public sector enterprises is free publicity for ministers and other political dignitaries. Newspapers in different languages are full of advertisements about inaugurations, milestones and conferences organized by public sector units. These advertisements always carry a series of photographs of ministers and party leaders. There are hoardings on streets, at frequent intervals, to mark any event in which leaders are participating (including personal visits to states where their parties are in power). There are bridges and arches with paintings of leaders expressing the gratitude of the public for launching all kinds of new projects and programmes. All expenses for such personal publicity are generally paid for by public sector enterprises, and occasionally by administrative ministries. India is unique in this respect as there is no other mature democracy in the world where personal publicity expenditure of this kind is borne by public sector units.

The powers conferred by virtue of controlling public enterprises are so enormous that any measure to reduce the discretionary powers of ministers in appointments, or to grant autonomy, or to reduce surplus staff invites immediate political opposition. Any such measure in respect of public enterprises is deemed as being against the 'public interest', even if this is not the case. Thus, according to media reports, the government was compelled to reverse its decision to authorize the Public Enterprises Selection Board (PESB) to recommend only one name for appointment as the chief executive officer (CEO) or executive director of a public sector undertaking (*Economic Times*, New Delhi, 7 March 2005). The PESB now has to offer more than one name of qualified candidates to the ministry for a decision. The reversal of the earlier decision had become necessary because of the reservations expressed by several ministers belonging to different parties in the coalition that the recommendation of only one name by PESB had in effect reduced them to the position of a 'rubber stamp'. They wanted more discretionary powers in the selection of chief executive officers (CEOs). It is obvious that such discretion is necessary for promoting the political interest of the ministers rather than for safeguarding the public interest or the interest of the economy as a whole.

I should make it clear that the issue here is not the public sector versus the private sector or the ideological predilections in favour of a market-dominated strategy vis-à-vis a State-dominated development strategy. Nor is it the case that all public enterprises perform inefficiently or that they do not contribute towards achieving the country's socio-economic goals. The point is simply that the exercise of political discretion in the functioning of public enterprises diminishes their potential contribution to the economy. There is no reasonable economic or ideological case for granting discretionary powers to political leaders in respect of appointments, management of commercial enterprises and allocation of resources. The socio-economic objectives can be more than adequately met by laying down appropriate policy guidelines, granting sufficient autonomy, and entrusting the responsibility for high level appointments, through transparent procedures, to official selection bodies.

Excessive Centralization

The pyramidal structure of political power has resulted in the over-centralization of administration rather than its decentralization. This has substantially increased the number of agencies, both horizontally and vertically, in the decision-making process, leading to administrative delays and lack of accountability for non-performance. No ministry wants to give up its power. At the same time, new ministries have to be created in order to accommodate aspirants from the majority party or from other parties in the coalition. Many of the new ministries have overlapping functions with existing ministries. In addition, there are ministries, offices and commissions with omnibus functions covering the entire government machinery, such as Finance, Planning, Personnel, and so on. This administrative structure at the Centre is replicated in the states. As most subjects are in the 'concurrent' list and/or involve the transfer of grants and loans from the Centre (e.g. power, irrigation, and rural development), multiple ministries and agencies at the Centre and states are involved in all administrative decision-making and the implementation of programmes.

At the bottom of the pyramid are the administrative agencies at the district, town, and village levels. Any work or programme at the level of the village or town is supposed to involve an elected body or a political representative in the decision-making process. Thus, as mentioned earlier, as early as 1994 (after the 73rd Amendment to the Constitution in 1993), all concerned states had passed their own acts for implementing the decision to set up Panchayati Raj Institutions (PRIs) with financial and administrative powers. However, states have not so far transferred most of the subjects or functions specified in the Constitutional amendment to PRIs. In order to exercise direct authority in areas reserved for panchayats, different ministries of state governments have also been inclined to create parallel structures at the local and district levels by forming committees under their control (such as village development committees in Haryana and watershed committees in Rajasthan and several other states). To make matters even more complicated, state laws generally permit state ministries and bureaucracies to wield powers of suspension and dismissal over elected PRIs. The retention of such powers over panchayat functionaries is believed to be in contravention of the intent of the 1993 Constitutional amendment.

The complexity of the governance structure and the exercise of political and bureaucratic control at multiple levels of the administrative machinery are vividly illustrated in the National Rural Employment Guarantee Act (NREGA), which was adopted in 2005. This Act is designed to provide guarantee of employment for a hundred days to every rural household in the country, and is perhaps one of the most important pieces of legislation in the socio-economic field since the founding of the Indian republic. While the objective of the Act is laudable, the bureaucratic structure for implementation of the programme is huge, involving several authorities at different levels of the political pyramid. Thus, in addition to at least five ministries of the Central government (e.g. Finance, Rural Development, Planning, Personnel and Panchayat) and their counterparts in each state (i.e. ten ministries at the Centre and the states), the Act envisages as many as ten or more agencies and committees at the Centre, state, district, block, and village levels for implementation, monitoring, evaluation, coordination, grievance redressal, and disbursement of funds. There is little doubt that the proposed gargantuan structure will be over-burdened with paper work, will work at cross purposes, and will fail to deliver the important objectives of the Act in a cost-effective manner within targeted dates in several states.

The reluctance to devolve political power and the desire to create more and more new agencies are combined with two other features of an overburdened administrative structure. First, virtually all legislation proposed by the government at the Centre or the states assigns residual and 'rule-making' powers to the concerned ministries. Such powers confer practically unlimited authority to make new rules, amend old rules and create public sector agencies under the Act. To acquire more power, in cases of doubt, the ministry can always propose adoption of a new Bill in place of an existing Act. Second, the higher the position of a person in the political hierarchy, the greater is the level of ostentatious display of power and authority. Thus, political leaders surround themselves with security personnel, preferably armed with visible weapons, and travel in a convoy of cars with red lights and sirens. At all public places, including airports and government offices, there is a special entry point or enclosure for so-called VVIPs (Very Very Important Persons) or VIPs (Very Important Persons). Such ostentation can, of course, be dismissed as frivolous. Unfortunately, however, it has an unintended effect on the politics of power. The loss of power, after elections or cabinet reshuffles, can lead to an acute sense of deprivation among VIPs and their families, which is not generally witnessed in other less ostentatious democracies. As a result, most political leaders and parties are willing to trade party loyalty or ideology in order to remain in office.

An interesting example of authoritarian powers that are sought to be conferred on a Central ministry is the Indian Medical Council (Amendment) Bill, 2005. The omnibus and unlimited powers, which are sought to be given to the Ministry of Health, include the following:

- In the discharge of its functions under this Act, the Indian Medical Council shall be guided by such directions, as may be given to it by the Central government.
- If any dispute arises between the Central government and the Council as to whether a question related to public interest or not, the decision of the Central government thereon shall be final.
- Further, the ministry will have the power to make any regulations or to amend or revoke any regulations for such period of time as it may specify.
- If the Council fails or neglects to comply with such orders within the specified period, the Central government may itself notify the regulations or amend or revoke the regulations made by the Council.
- The Central government may by notification also dissolve the Executive Committee or the Medical Council or such other committees at its discretion.

- After dissolution of the Executive Committee, the ministry will have the power to appoint whoever it considers appropriate to exercise the functions of the Executive Committee for the specified period.
- The ministry will have the power to remove the President or the Vice-President or any member from the Council at its discretion.

With such unlimited powers, it is easy to visualize how much damage can be inflicted on the functioning of an autonomous body in the critical field of medicine by a determined political head of a ministry, if he or she so wishes. With frequent changes in government in the last seventeen years (upto 2006), India has had eight different Ministers of Health. These ministers had different orientations and different views on what was right and what was wrong (in fact, as recently reported in the press, a former Minister of Health is currently being investigated by the CBI for some improprieties). With unlimited powers at his or her disposal, a new minister can easily change the policy introduced by his or her predecessor or impose his or her will on the entire medical profession in the country.

In conclusion, I must reiterate that there are some persons of exceptional talent and integrity in India's politics, who serve the country selflessly to promote the welfare of the public in general. There are also cases where political leaders have willingly renounced political power rather than seek it. It is also true that most other democracies, including those in Europe and the United States, exhibit similar characteristics of power play as India. However, what is different here is the extent of economic power, and domination over commercial activity by government—directly or indirectly. It is this immense commercial power in the hands of political leaders which makes India different from other mature democracies. As mentioned before, while democracy is its own reward, and is precious to all citizens, there are costs attached to the unbridled exercise of power at the political level. In this connection, the observation of the recent high-level National Commission to Review the Working of the Constitution (Chairman: Justice M.N. Venkatachaliah) speaks for itself:

> A fundamental breach of the Constitutional faith on the part of governments and their method of governance lies in the neglect of the people who are the ultimate source of all political authority. Public servants and institutions are not alive to the basic imperative that they are servants of the people meant to serve them. The dignity of the individual enshrined in the Constitution has remained an unredeemed pledge. There is, thus, a loss of faith in the governments and governance. Citizens see their governments besieged by uncontrollable events and are losing faith in institutions. Society is unable to cope up with current events. (Venkatachaliah Commission 2002)[12]

References

1. R.F. Kennedy (1964), 'The Pursuit of Justice', as quoted in *The International Thesaurus of Quotations*, New York: Harper and Row, 1970.

2. A. Schleifer and R.W. Vishny (1998), *The Grabbing Hand: Government Pathologies and their Cures*, Cambridge, Mass.: Harvard University Press.

3. A.K. Dixit (2006), *Lawlessness and Economics: Alternative Modes of Governance*, New Delhi: Oxford University Press.

4. World Bank (2005), *The Political Economy of Gram Panchayats in South India: Results and Policy Conclusions from a Research Project*, Washington, DC, mimeo.

5. T. Besley et al. (2005), 'Political Selection and the Quality of Government: Evidence from South India', paper presented at the Conference on the State of Panchayats and the Way Forward, New Delhi, 16–18 December 2005.

6. *Indian Express*, 'Democracy for Sale in TN, Highest Bidders Get Panchayat Posts', New Delhi, 26 September 2006.

7. Reserve Bank of India (2005), *State Finances: A Study of Budgets of 2005–06*, Mumbai.

8. Planning Commission, Government of India (2005), *Performance Evaluation of Targeted Public Distribution System (TPDS)*, New Delhi, mimeo.

9. M. Carter (2006), 'We Can Only Do Our Bit', *Indian Express*, New Delhi, 5 April 2006.

10. M. Olson (1965), *The Logic of Collective Action*, Cambridge, Mass.: Harvard University Press.

11. G.S. Becker (1983), 'A Theory of Competition Among Pressure Groups for Political Influence', *Quarterly Journal of Economics*, June-September 1983.

12. *Report of the National Commission to Review the Working of the Constitution* (2002), Delhi: Universal Law Publishing Company, p. 50.

THREE

The Corruption of Politics

Long ago, at the height of British imperial power in India and other colonies, Lord Acton had observed, 'Power tends to corrupt; absolute power corrupts absolutely.'[1] In an independent and democratic India, while political power still confers enormous leverage on those who are in a position to exercise it, the extent of power—and the corruption associated with it—is not absolute. The Constitution has put several checks and balances on the exercise of power by those in authority. The judiciary is independent and accessible to the public at large for redressal of their grievances. The media is also free and active. Cases of corruption and instances of the arbitrary exercise of power are frequently exposed in the print and electronic media after investigation by journalists. In cases where there is sufficient *prima facie* evidence of corruption, there are well-established procedures for official investigation and prosecution. In addition, the Parliament of India and the legislative assemblies in the states have their own privileges committees (and/or ethics committees), which have the power to censure, and in extreme cases to expel, their members for corruption and violations of established norms of behaviour. A recent case in which Parliament unanimously exercised its authority to expel some of its members for corruption, on the recommendation of its committees, was in December 2005 in the famous MPLAD i.e. Members of Parliament Local Area Development case (involving acceptance of bribes in the allocation of funds).

At the same time, it is also a fact that the number of cases where action has been taken to convict those charged with corruption and other criminal practices is extremely small. Indeed, an increasing number of persons with criminal records are now contesting elections and acquiring political power in order to delay or prevent conviction. Thus, statistics compiled by the Association for Democratic Reforms (ADR) for elections to the Lok Sabha in 2004 show that, out of the 3,182 candidates surveyed, as many as 518 candidates, cutting across all political parties, had criminal antecedents.[2] Out of these 518 candidates, as many as 115 were elected to the Lok Sabha (which has 543 seats in all). Some of the elected members with criminal antecedents, belonging to different parties, also became members of the Union Cabinet or other public organizations.

The position was no different when another combination of parties had formed the government in the previous elections. Persons with long-standing criminal records have been free to contest elections and assume political office because technically, as per the law, they are presumed to be 'innocent until proven guilty'. In view of lengthy legal procedures and multiple levels of appeal, persons charged with committing even the most heinous and grave offences can remain free and continue to contest elections over an indefinite period. Political power provides additional protection against conviction for past offences because of control over government agencies responsible for investigation and prosecution.

In view of the choice of a political career by persons with a criminal past, it is often said that in India and some other democracies, 'a person would rather be in politics than in jail'. The ease with which individuals with known records of corruption and other crimes are selected by political parties to contest elections partly explains the low public esteem in which politicians are generally held in India. Thus, another survey by the Association for Democratic Reform revealed that, on a scale of zero to ten, in terms of honesty and integrity, politicians enjoyed a very low average score of 3.21. In terms of their contribution to society and their effectiveness in carrying out their duties, people in political life scored only 3.44 and 3.74 respectively.[3]

At this point, it is important to emphasize that the spread of corruption is not confined to politicians alone. Nor is it correct to presume that most politicians are personally corrupt or have criminal records. Indeed, there are several people in political office who have an unimpeachable record of integrity and high performance in office. The above scores (which are by no means entirely representative) are only indicative of the extent of corruption and criminal behaviour in political life. Several other professions, including the administrative services, industry, and commerce, also suffer from the same disease. There is sufficient evidence of what some writers have referred to as the 'vertical integration of corruption' at different tiers of the government hierarchy—elected politicians, higher bureaucracy and lower bureaucracy.[4] In addition to vertical integration, there is also a horizontal spread of corruption among other public institutions, including parts of the judiciary, parts of the media and some independent professions. The spread of corruption, horizontally and vertically, in practically all segments of the country is the primary reason why prevention and control of corruption have become so difficult. It has also led to a general acceptance of corruption as a 'necessary evil' in Indian society.

A person no less than the Prime Minister of India recently observed that: 'The country's justice delivery system appears to be on the verge of collapse . . . the manner in which some cases are being prosecuted, particularly where cases fail because witnesses turn hostile or change their evidence, is causing concern to ever increasing sections of society . . . instances of corruption have now begun to surface in our judicial system also.' These observations of the prime minister were made at the All-India Conference of Chief Ministers and Chief Justices in March 2006, and were echoed by several other participants, including the Chief Justice of India.

Referring to some recent cases of corruption and miscarriage of justice, the chief justice said:

The public outrage over the failure of the criminal
justice system in some high-profile cases must shake
us all up into the realization that something needs
to be urgently done to revamp the whole process,
though steering clear of knee-jerk reactions,
remembering that law is a serious business.[5]

This is the current state of affairs in India, according
to the heads of both the government and the judiciary.
We will discuss some of the issues relating to corruption
in politics in greater detail below, including the reasons
why corruption is now as widespread as it is.

Causes of Corruption

Shleifer and Vishny (1998) have put forward an
interesting analysis of the causes of corruption under
the catchy title of the 'grabbing hand' model of
political behaviour. Under this model, contrary to the
assumptions made in the traditional development
literature, the economic policies pursued by political
leaders in authoritarian as well as democratic regimes
are not necessarily designed to maximize social welfare.
People in power prefer to pursue their own separate
political objectives. According to Shleifer and Vishny,
'In authoritarian regimes leaders use their powers to
keep themselves in office, to direct resources to political
supporters, to destroy political challenges, and to
enrich themselves, often at the expense of public
welfare. Democracies often induce politicians with
more public-spirited incentives, in part because they
need to be re-elected, but democratically elected
politicians typically do not maximize social welfare

either.'[6] In democracies, according to their analysis, interest groups and lobbies tend to exercise substantial influence on political decisions because politicians need votes and monetary contributions in order to get re-elected.

The extent of corruption and its causes in different democracies, or for that matter in autocratic regimes, is, of course, not the same. In India, in the early post-Independence years, there was hardly any corruption among political leaders. In a few cases, where there was suspicion of special favours being shown to some industrial houses, the ministers concerned chose to resign rather than continue in office, even though there was no direct evidence of personal corruption (for example, in the famous Mundra case in 1957 involving T.T. Krishnamachari, the then finance minister). Unlike several other democracies, Indian democracy was a direct result of a non-violent nationalist struggle against colonial rule, spread over several decades. The nationalist struggle was led by political leaders who had made enormous personal sacrifices and had set inspiring examples of 'simple living and high thinking' for the country. People in political power were not only expected to be incorruptible but also appear to be so to the public at large.

Gradually and imperceptibly, however, the position has changed, and India is now regarded as one of the most corrupt democracies in the world. According to the widely quoted Transparency International's corruption perception index (CPI), in the early years of the twenty-first century, India was ranked as having one of the highest levels of corruption in the world. India's rank was higher than non-democratic countries like China. It was also substantially higher than other East Asian countries like Japan, Malaysia and South Korea.[7]

The causes of the sharp rise in India's position among the world's most politically corrupt nations are multiple. The most important among them is the immense political power of the 'coalitions of special interests', which was further strengthened by the post-Independence strategy of centralized control over allocation of the nation's resources. After independence from colonial rule, there were valid reasons for India opting for a State-dominated development strategy. India was abysmally poor, and there had virtually been no growth in the national income during the first half of the twentieth century. An important reason for India's economic stagnation, despite abundant natural resources, was believed to be the colonial patterns of trade whereby India was an exporter of cheap primary goods and an importer of expensive industrial products. Against this background, there was unanimity among nationalist intellectuals, political leaders, and industrialists about the preferred direction of economic strategy after Independence (Chandra 2004).[8] The need for the government to occupy the commanding heights of the economy and to lead from the top received further support from the astounding success of the Soviet Union in emerging as a centre of political and industrial power within a very short period.

While the reasons for adopting a centrally directed strategy of development were understandable against the background of colonial rule, it soon became clear that the actual results of this strategy were far below expectations. Instead of showing high growth, high public savings and a high degree of self-reliance, India was actually showing one of the lowest rates of growth in the developing world, with rising public deficits and periodic balance-of-payments crises. Despite poor results, which had become evident by the mid-1960s, when India was plunged into a deep balance-of-payments crisis accompanied by food insecurity because of droughts, there was no change in the development strategy for another two decades. There was further deterioration in governance and extension of controls to virtually all areas of the nation's economy in order to save foreign exchange and other scarce resources.

Beginning in the early 1980s, there was a loosening of licensing and import controls. The process of reforms gathered momentum after another major crisis in 1991. However, as is well known, despite reforms the administrative and procedural hassles at multiple levels of the government continue to flourish even now. Political leaders are still gaining from their control over the resources of public sector enterprises, their power to regulate the activities of large private sector enterprises, their power to fix prices of agricultural and industrial goods, and their ability to provide subsidies and incur fiscal deficits. Workers in the organized sector, in both the public and the private sectors, continue to gain from immense powers and political patronage enjoyed by them. Bureaucrats gain from opportunities for corruption at different levels of the administration and from the statutorily guaranteed security of their jobs. Private sector entrepreneurs and contractors are also important beneficiaries because of their ability to influence government decisions in their favour through the preferential allocation of resources and contracts, particularly during elections (which are taking place with increasing frequency).

Government fiscal budgets are large, but, as we have noted in the previous chapter, because of large salary bills, multiplicity of programmes, and the many agencies involved in implementing them, there is a severe shortage of budgetary resources in meeting demands for government expenditure. The power to allocate these scarce resources lies with the political leaders in power, who tend to cater to their own party interests and other special interests that are in a position to help them during and after elections. Land and other public resources are scarce, and the power of allocation of such resources among competing private interests lies largely with the government. This provides further scope for political and bureaucratic corruption at different levels of the administration.

In addition to the power of special interests, another important cause of political corruption is the high cost of contesting elections. In a multi-tier democracy like India's, all citizens are free to fight elections either on behalf of a political party or as independents. Elections are held at different times at various levels of the political structure. In the era of coalition governments, elections at the state and Central levels have also become more frequent than was the case earlier. Political leaders are, therefore, virtually in a campaign mode during most of the year on behalf of themselves or other candidates nominated by their parties. In view of India's large population, at the higher levels of the political system, the constituencies are also large, indeed larger than those found in any other established democracy in Europe, Asia or America. Although the size of the constituencies across the country varies greatly, depending on geography and population density, on an average the number of voters in a constituency for elections to the Lok Sabha is more than one million people, spread over a large geographical area. In the electronic age, the cost of campaigning for elected office is also high, particularly for publicity, transport and subsistence of political workers.

In order to make elections affordable and accessible to parties or individuals who do not have very large funds, the Election Commission has put limits on the maximum expenditure by a candidate in a constituency. There are also prescribed rules for political parties to declare their assets as well as the contributions that they may receive. These rules have laudable objectives. However, in practice these have had some perverse results. The rules are scrupulously adhered to on paper, but there is strong evidence that actual campaign expenditure has not been contained. Excess expenditure over the prescribed limits is being financed through two other sources: (a) supply of free campaign goods and services directly by unnamed contributors; and (b) financial contributions to the party or to candidates in cash and 'undeclared' funds.

The National Election Audit for 1999, conducted by the Centre for the Study of Developing Societies (CSDS), New Delhi, shows that in that year the average election expenditure incurred by a victorious candidate in a Lok Sabha constituency was about Rs 8.5 million. This was nearly six times higher than the then permissible limit of Rs 1.5 million. In 2003, the expenditure ceiling was raised to Rs 2.5 million. It is likely that in the 2004 national elections, the actual expenditure by a winning candidate was again several times higher than the revised limit. It may be mentioned here that the coverage of expenditure included in the legally fixed limits is also ambiguous, and that the actual expenditure can easily exceed these limits without any problem. Thus, Explanation I, Section 77(1) of the Representation of People's Act, 1951 allows political parties and their supporters to spend any amount in a given constituency—over and above the expenditure ceilings applicable to individual candidates—provided there is no direct coordination with, or mention of, the candidates.[9] This legal loophole permits any candidate to spend indirectly as much as he or she wishes through a political party or through another person.

The need to raise large funds for financing elections has made political corruption widely acceptable and unavoidable in most constituencies across the country. There are, of course, some exceptions. Persons with high political standing, popularity or personal wealth do not necessarily have to rely on undeclared sources of funds to fight and win elections. However, in most parties, such persons are in a small minority.

To make corruption a less compelling factor in the need to raise funds for elections, it is now imperative for India to introduce a fair and equitable scheme for the State funding of elections. We shall return to this subject in a later chapter on the agenda for political reforms.

The procedure for elections to the Rajya Sabha, i.e. the Council of States, was radically changed in 2003 by amending the Representation of the People Act, 1951 in both Houses of Parliament. The domicile requirement for a candidate to be elected from a particular state was removed, and the provision for secret ballot by members of the state legislatures was replaced by 'open' voting. Thus, a person resident anywhere in India can now be elected to the Rajya Sabha from any state. If a party has the requisite number of votes in the legislature to elect a member to the Rajya Sabha, the members of that legislature have no option but to vote for the party's candidate.

The amendments in the election rules were justified by the then ruling coalition on the ground that some elected members were, in any case, making false declarations about their domicile in a particular state, and that the earlier provisions for secret ballot were encouraging cross-voting by members for wrong reasons, such as bribes. Unfortunately, irrespective of the intentions behind these amendments, the actual effect has been to strengthen the grip of a few leaders of political parties in deciding who should represent a particular state in one of the highest forums of India's federal democracy. So far, many of the candidates selected for elections to the Rajya Sabha by different parties have impressive credentials. At the same time, there is also evidence that any person with sufficient resources and/or personal clout can find a berth in the Rajya Sabha with support from one or more parties from some state or the other, even if he/she has no connection with that state. During elections to the Rajya Sabha in March 2006, the importance of monetary considerations in securing party nominations was widely reported in the media. The following headlines from three different daily newspapers speak for themselves:

- 'Road to Rajya Sabha: Money Can Buy You a Seat', *Times of India*, New Delhi, 17 March 2006.
- 'Moneybags on Prowl in RS Polls', *Economic Times*, New Delhi, 18 March 2006.
- 'Why Office is Profit, Profit is Office', *Indian Express*, 26 March 2006.

The amendments to the rules for election to the Rajya Sabha have no doubt curbed the scope for corrupt practices by a few individual members of a state assembly. Unfortunately, in practice, these amendments have also caused immense damage to the reputation of an august House of Parliament in the public mind. All electoral powers of the Rajya Sabha are now concentrated in the hands of the leaders of political parties, some of whom, as widely reported in the media, are inclined to use these powers to raise additional funds for themselves or their parties from aspiring candidates.

As is well known, members of Parliament and state legislatures enjoy various perquisites such as housing, free travel, and constituency allowance, in addition to a basic salary. In a large country like India, where most of the legislators are not permanent residents of Delhi or other state capitals, there is perhaps a good case to be made for providing such facilities. The scale of facilities available to a member, however, increases dramatically when he or she becomes a minister in the government or a holder of any other high public office. Ostentatious displays of power as a 'VIP' (Very Important Person) and 'VVIP' (Very Very Important Person!) have become an essential part of the perquisites of an office holder in a democracy which, many years ago, was established on the principles of simplicity and sacrifice by the representatives of the people.

As mentioned in the previous chapter, conspicuous consumption, high living and ostentation by so-called 'public servants' could be dismissed as frivolous and unworthy of serious comment but for the fact that these have had a most unfortunate effect on party politics. The sense of deprivation and loss of social status in losing office, and all the paraphernalia and manpower associated with it, among members of a party have important behavioural implications for all political parties, particularly small regional parties. In India, family ties are also strong in determining a person's position in the social hierarchy. As such, the sense of deprivation affects not only those who participate in politics directly but also all those who are associated or connected with them. The compulsions and pressures to remain in power are, therefore, enormous. This partly explains why political parties are quick to change sides or split into smaller formations in the event of a threat to the stability of a coalition government. Inducements to join new coalitions (or to remain in existing coalitions) are commonplace. New devices have also been put in place to prevent members from changing sides during negotiations and a party's bid for power (such as, collective isolation of all members in a separate hotel and/or close monitoring of their daily activities, including phone calls).

The monetary salary paid to ordinary members of Parliament/legislatures and to holders of public offices is relatively small in comparison with the high costs to the public exchequer of non-monetary perquisites provided to them. This is supposed to be a tribute to the hallowed tradition of 'simple living' by persons in public life. The contemporary reality is, however, very different as many successful politicians also incur large personal expenditures for themselves, their families, and their retinues. Unless they have independent sources of income from industry, real estate, and other professions, this expenditure has to be met through the supply of 'free goods' and undeclared monetary compensation to them for providing special access to government contracts and public resources (such as the allocation of Local Area Development funds, recently reported in the media).

In addition to the above factors, there are, of course, other causes of political corruption, such as personal greed and the desire for the accumulation of assets or the need for seeking favours from others who are more powerful. However, these factors are also widely prevalent in other professions and sectors, and do not require a separate discussion here.

Costs to Society

In view of the spread of corruption to all walks of life in India, and its pervasive impact on society, the National Human Rights Commission convened a high-level conference in May 2006 to consider various aspects of the problem. The conference was inaugurated by the President of India. It was addressed by several eminent persons who highlighted the adverse consequences of corruption on India's development and protection of basic human rights. In his opening remarks, the Chairperson of the Commission, and former Chief Justice of India, Dr A.S. Anand, spoke about the areas of particular concern:

> Corruption has become all pervasive and is eating into the vitals of the society. It directly contributes to inequalities in income, status and opportunities. It remains one of the biggest threats to 'full human development' and 'human rights for all'. It undermines the rule of law. It distorts the development process and also poses a grave threat to human security. Corruption is not a new phenomenon. What is new and worrying is the magnitude and size of corruption. It has spread its tentacles to every sphere of national life. It is one of the biggest threats to development. It can tear the very fabric of the society and, in fact, it is doing so. Corruption benefits the rich and the well-to-do. It enriches the rich and disproportionately affects the poor, the unprotected and the underprivileged and thereby it deepens their deprivation.[10]

As pointed out by Justice Anand and other speakers at the conference, the worst impact of corruption is on the poor. The fact that the rich gain and the poor lose as a result of corrupt practices has also been confirmed by several empirical studies on the effects of corruption on the delivery of public services. Cross-country studies suggest that the corruption perception index, on an average, is higher in poor countries such as India, because of the large proportion of people living below the poverty line (Abed and Davoodi 2002)[11]. Government expenditures are inflated and wasteful projects and programmes are taken up, including the purchase of spurious drugs and unsafe equipment, thus posing hazards to safety, life, and longevity. There is widespread diversion of good-quality essential goods (such as food for the poor) where these are distributed by government agencies to private retailers. The poor are unable to secure adequate food or essential health services, and are thus unable to benefit from government subsidies provided on their behalf. This is an important cause of the persistence of poverty in many low-income countries and for the accentuation of inequality in an already unequal society.

An important finding of empirical research, which is not widely appreciated in poor countries, is that the choice of projects and programmes by many government agencies is often driven by their potential for corruption and illicit gains rather than for their contribution to national output or the real rate of return on such projects. In addition to a strong political bias in favour of launching unproductive and high-cost projects in uneconomic locations, there is also an inherent bias against spending, maintenance and on human capital formation. These activities generally have lower scope for illegitimate monetary transfers to intermediaries than setting up new projects (Tanzi and Davoodi 2002).[12]

A reduction in political and administrative corruption can significantly increase investment and the investment–income ratio, and thus enhance growth and promote a better distribution of income. According to Mauro (1995), in a country where corruption is widespread, a reduction in corruption by, say, 50 per cent can increase the growth rate by nearly 1.5 percentage points.[13] While no independent estimate has been made for the growth-reducing effects of government and private corruption in India, my rough calculations, based on Mauro's econometric model and anecdotal evidence, is that it could be even higher—nearly 2 percentage points or so. In other words, all things remaining the same, if there were no corruption, India's growth rate would have been nearly 8 per cent per annum in the 1980s and 1990s, rather than close to 6 per cent.

Another interesting finding of empirical research is that the adverse economic effects of corruption are more pronounced on small enterprises and on the overall growth of employment in the economy. Thus, a survey of 3,000 enterprises across twenty transition economies, covering all regions, found that corruption and anti-competitive practices were perceived as the most difficult obstacles by start-up firms (EBRD 1999).[14] For large enterprises, corruption often increases profits as it allows them to enjoy monopoly rents and scale economies. For small enterprises, corruption

raises costs and reduces profits because they have to
make payments that do not contribute to productivity
or output but are necessary for their survival. In order
to avoid undue harassment, bribes that may amount
to a substantial portion of the operating costs of such
enterprises, have to be paid to meet the demands of a
host of inspectors working in concert with each other.
This becomes an important cause of sickness of small
industries, requiring further assistance from local
governments or banks, which in turn affects their
viability.

Corruption is also an important cause of fiscal
drain and higher inflation in developing societies.
There is strong empirical evidence that countries with
high levels of corruption tend to have lower collection
of tax revenues in relation to their national incomes
(Friedman et al. 2000).[15] Corruption has a statistically
significant negative correlation with receipts from
personal income taxes since private negotiations with
tax inspectors is a common practice in many developing
countries, including India. It is estimated that a one
point increase in corruption is associated with as
much as a 0.63 per cent decline in receipts from
individual income taxes. Indirect tax collections,
particularly revenue from customs duties and excise
duties, are also highly sensitive to the degree of
corruption. It has also been found that the higher the
level of duties, and the greater the variability in tax
rates (depending on the type of goods), the higher will
be the scope for corruption and the accompanying
revenue drain. As rates increase and corruption rises,
the tax system as a whole becomes less progressive.

This phenomenon and the negative circular relationship between corruption and investment help explain the 'poverty trap' in which many low-income countries, including India, find themselves. This also presents an important dilemma for public policy and development strategy. In countries with poor infrastructure, particularly in rural areas with a high incidence of poverty, public investment is the essential instrument through which productivity and income levels can be raised. At the same time, the higher the level of public investment in relation to GDP, the higher is likely to be the level of corruption and its negative effects on growth. The solution thus becomes the problem.

Taken as a whole, there is no doubt that, contrary to popular perception, corruption is a major cause of economic deprivation, high incidence of poverty, and fiscal disempowerment in developing countries, including India. The costs to society as a whole are disproportionately high, much higher than the benefits of corruption enjoyed by the few belonging to the upper-income groups. Solutions for mitigating or reducing the effects of corruption in a poor society are, however, by no means easy because of the power of special interests. A multi-pronged approach is necessary, including reduction in the role of politicians and bureaucrats in the implementation of programmes, introducing greater transparency, reducing judicial delays, and increasing the accountability of the government to the people for actual performance in the delivery of services. We will return to some of these issues later.

A Career of Choice

At this point, it is also necessary to recognize that while political corruption is widespread, its causes are manifold and its costs to society are high, not all elected politicians are personally and voluntarily corrupt. There are a fairly large number of individuals at different levels of the political hierarchy who are known for their integrity and who pursue their political careers without enriching themselves or their families. At the higher levels, in state legislatures and in Parliament, there are several members with highly impressive professional credentials who are successful lawyers, doctors and accountants. Scions of industrial and business families, with sufficient wealth of their own, are also represented. Some of them may use their positions to advance their business interests or provide financial support to political parties but, by and large, they are on the sidelines of politics rather than active participants.

However, what is troubling about the current situation is that the mix of representation of good and bad in politics seems to be changing in favour of the latter. Entry into politics continues to be free and competitive at the ground level. However, a belief is gaining ground that in order to make progress in politics, there is no option but to indulge in sycophancy, corruption, and the accumulation of illicit wealth. This is partly a result of the emergence of a large number of political parties in different regions with narrow casteist, religious or populist agendas. In most parties, including national parties with a significant presence in different parts of the country, inner-party democracy is conspicuous by its absence. Most of them, with some honourable exceptions, are led by a few leaders who decide on nominees for elections at various levels, and appointments to public offices (when they are in power). In this situation, sycophancy and subservience to the wishes of party leaders are unavoidable.

A related issue of concern for the future is the universal acceptance of corruption as an unavoidable feature of political life in India. Even if a political leader or an ordinary member of a legislature is personally incorruptible and conforms to the highest standards of probity, he or she is still willing to accept corruption as unavoidable and tends to accept persons with established criminal records to be active in politics. This phenomenon explains why an increasing number of persons with a criminal past are now able to get elected to legislatures and get appointed to high public offices, even though the top leaders in the government may themselves be incorruptible.

Against this background, although entry into politics is open to everyone, and any Indian citizen is free to fight an election or launch a political party, persons who can pursue a successful career in politics without adequate means of their own are becoming rarer. The public in general, including social activists, are relatively indifferent to the quality and qualifications of the persons who are elected as their representatives. A view is gaining ground that all politicians are alike, personally corrupt and insensitive to public interest. As such, it does not really matter who gets elected or what politicians actually do. It is also believed that, in any case, the Indian economy is on a high growth path. As long as politicians do not interfere with private investment initiatives, it is considered immaterial whether they are corrupt and have criminal backgrounds. Given the vast size of India's population and its diverse economy, the impact of the activities of a relatively small number of politicians on the total economy is presumed to be small.

Unfortunately, the above assumptions about the impact of politics on a country's economy or its society are not valid. There is sufficient empirical evidence to show that, in developing countries in particular, the nature and cohesiveness of political behaviour have a decisive influence on growth, employment, poverty alleviation and domestic stability. If politics is generally corrupt and/or non-responsive to the public interest, a country's prospects are bound to be adversely affected. Signs of discontent and lawlessness are already emerging in large parts of India because of political apathy and administrative inaction. According to the Government of India's own estimates, one-third to one-fourth of the country is now under the influence of Naxalite organizations, without any effective presence of state governments in the maintenance of law and order.

A recent study on the impact of political institutions and policy-making processes on economic outcomes in thirteen Latin American countries has concluded that:

Important features of public policies depend crucially on the ability of political actors to reach and enforce inter-temporal agreements: that is, to cooperate. In political environments that facilitate such agreements, public policies will tend to be of higher quality, less sensitive to political shocks, and more adaptable to changing economic and social conditions. In contrast, in settings that hinder cooperation, policies will be either too unstable (subject to political swings) or too inflexible (unable to adapt to socio-economic shocks); they will tend to be poorly coordinated; and investments in State capabilities will tend to be lower.[16]

Drawing on the diverse experiences of Latin American countries, many of whom have similar political institutions, the above study has suggested that co-operative and positive outcomes are more likely if:

- There are good 'aggregation technologies' so that the number of actors with a direct impact on the policy-making process is relatively small.
- There are well-institutionalized arenas for political exchanges.
- Key actors have long-time horizons.
- There are credible enforcement mechanisms, such as an independent judiciary and a strong bureaucracy to which the implementation of certain public policies can be delegated.

As we shall see in later chapters, none of the above conditions is met fully in the Indian context. Since 1989, the term of office of the government, on an average, has been relatively short. There have been seven heads of governments, formed by different coalitions of parties. The political exchange among different parties in the government and those in the

Opposition has been highly discordant, and proceedings in both Houses of Parliament and in several state legislatures have been disrupted frequently. The bureaucracy has been politicized. There have been large-scale transfers of administrative personnel with every change in the holders of ministerial offices. The number of parties involved in policy-making has increased substantially. There has also been a severe erosion in the principle of collective responsibility of the Cabinet for policy decisions.

India, of course, has a much longer experience in the working of its democratic Constitution, and its political institutions are more firmly established than those in many Latin American countries. The parliamentary form of government, where the executive is a part of the legislature and enjoys the support of a majority of members, avoids conflicts in the law-making process experienced by some countries with a presidential form of government. The legislature in these countries has separate and independent powers, and the legislation proposed by the executive branch can be rejected by a majority vote. While the Indian system has its advantages, in the light of the more recent experience with successive coalition governments in India, it is also clear that there is need to consider measures to further strengthen the process of policy formulation at the political level and to enforce the accountability of the executive for its performance (see Chapter 6).

An important requirement for making politics a career of choice for individuals of modest means with a devotion to public service is to make the internal processes of decision-making in political parties more democratic. Under the present system, all decisions within a party, including the selection of candidates for elections or for nomination to public offices, are made by a few leaders. At the lower levels, such as village panchayats, entry into politics is still relatively easy and competitive. However, at the higher levels of the political pyramid, entry and promotions are highly selective and subjective. The number of party positions and seats in legislatures (including Parliament) are relatively few, and the selection of candidates is entirely at the discretion of party leaders. Political parties also do not maintain an accessible list of their registered members in different constituencies across the country. Registered members pay a nominal fee for membership, but have no voice in the selection of candidates for elections.

In order to test the popularity of alternative candidates for election to state and federal legislatures, the United States and some other democracies have introduced a system of primary elections. This procedure has the advantage of encouraging more than one member of a party to prove his or her popularity among all the registered members of that party. Those who are elected in the primaries automatically become the candidates of their parties in the final elections for the legislatures as well as for the presidency.

The above example is illustrative of a broad-based and democratic system for choosing candidates for elections to higher offices of the State. The leaders of political parties do play a role in influencing voter choices during election campaigns, but they are not the final authority in deciding who can get promoted to higher levels in politics. The above-mentioned system of primary elections is not without its faults or problems, but it is certainly more open and democratic and less subservient to the wishes of a few party leaders. It is to be hoped that, in the not too distant future, keeping in view the larger interests of the country, political parties in India would also consider ways and means of introducing inner-party democracy in their functioning and, if necessary, bringing about suitable legislation to that effect.

References

1. Lord Acton, *Letter to Mandell Creighton*, 5 April 1887, London, UK.

2. Association for Democratic Reforms (2006), *Proceedings of the Third National Workshop on Electoral and Political Party Reforms*, 11-12 February 2006, Patna, p. 5.

3. Association for Democratic Reforms (2006), *Proceedings of the Third National Workshop on Electoral and Political Party Reforms*, 11-12 February 2006, Patna, p. 15.

4. S. Guhan and S. Paul (1997), *Corruption in India: Agenda for Action*, Delhi: Vision Books.

5. As reported in the *Indian Express*, New Delhi, 12 March 2006.

6. A. Schleifer and R.W. Vishny (1998), *The Grabbing Hand: Government Pathologies and their Cures*, Cambridge, Mass.: Harvard University Press.

7. Transparency International (2006), *The Global Corruption Report*, London: Pluto Press.

8. B. Chandra (2004), 'The Colonial Legacy', in B. Jalan (ed.), *The Indian Economy: Problems and Prospects*, New Delhi: Penguin.

9. V.K. Chand (ed.) (2006), *Reinventing Public Service Delivery in India: Selected Case Studies*, The World Bank and Sage Publications.

10. Justice Dr A.S. Anand (2006), *Welcome Address at National Conference on Corruption*, 9 May 2006, National Human Rights Commission, New Delhi.

11. G.T. Abed and H.R. Davoodi (2002), 'Corruption, Structural Reforms, and Economic Performance' in G.T. Abed and S. Gupta (eds.) *Governance, Corruption and Economic Performance*, International Monetary Fund, Washington, DC.

12. V. Tanzi and H.R. Davoodi (2002), 'Corruption, Public Investment, and Growth' in Abed and Gupta (eds.) *Governance, Corruption and Economic Performance*, International Monetary Fund, Washington, DC.

13. P. Mauro (1995), 'Corruption and Growth', *Quarterly Journal of Economics*, August 1995.

14. European Bank for Reconstruction and Development (1999), *Ten Years of Transition*, London.

15. E. Friedman et al. (2000), 'Dodging the Grabbing Hand: The Determinants of Unofficial Activity in 69 Countries', *Journal of Public Economics*, vol. 76.

16. Inter-American Development Bank (2006), *The Politics of Policies: Economic and Social Progress in Latin America*, David Rockefeller Center for Latin American Studies, Harvard University, USA, p. 19.

FOUR

The Diminishing Role
of Parliament

The Prime Minister of India, in a speech at an awards function in April 2006, echoed a sentiment about India's democracy that is widely shared among its admirers all over the world. He said, 'Our democracy was not built on the simple principle of the rule of the majority. It was, I believe, built on the idea of Unity in Diversity. That is the most important idea that Gandhiji and Panditji gave us. The idea of building a consensus. It is a great liberal idea which rejects extremes and extremism.'[1] Nowhere else is India's achievement in realizing the goal of 'unity in diversity', and its efforts to build a consensus, more visible than in the two Houses of Parliament.

The Parliament of India is truly representative of the vast economic, social, regional, and religious diversity of India. All income classes are represented, from the richest industrialist to the poorest farmer. All castes and all regions find equitable representation depending on their size, population and electoral popularity. Members belong to different religions, and can openly and freely espouse their beliefs, irrespective of their numbers. In the midst of this great diversity, there is also unity. Every member has a single vote and an equal right to intervene in the debate independently or on behalf of a party. The time and space allotted to party or non-party members is also equitably distributed depending on their numbers. Ministers speak on behalf of the government, but have no special privileges or ostentatious perquisites or attendants inside the House. Any member is free to interrupt, shout, or otherwise disrupt the proceedings of the House, irrespective of seniority, and is subject only to the directions of the Chair inside the House. While there is discussion and debate on important matters, and there are strong political differences among the parties within and outside the government, most legislative proposals and official resolutions are adopted without dissent.

Any reader of India's rich history of parliamentary proceedings has much to be proud of. The Parliament is the supreme forum of India's democracy, and represents the will of the people and their different identities. Except for some brief aberrations (such as during the period of the Emergency, 1975–77), successive governments have also been sensitive to the views of Parliament on issues of high national policy, foreign affairs, and defence.

While all this is true, below the surface, in recent years, there has been a subtle change in the role of Parliament which is not evident at first glance. All citizens who follow the news in the media or who watch parliamentary proceedings are aware of, and perhaps disappointed by, the frequent disruptions that now occur in the two Houses. The concern with the functioning of India's Parliament and state legislatures in recent years was also voiced by the National Commission to Review the Working of the Constitution:

> If there is a sense of unease with the way the Parliament and the State legislatures are functioning, it may be due to a decline in recent years in both the quantity and quality of work done by them. Over the years the number of days on which the houses sit to transact legislative and other business has come down very significantly. Even the relatively fewer days on which the houses meet are often marked by unseemly incidents, including use of force to intimidate opponents, shouting and shutting out of debate and discussion resulting in frequent adjournments. There is increasing concern about the decline of Parliament's falling standards of debate, erosion of the moral authority and prestige of the supreme tribune of the people.[2]

My purpose in drawing attention to the diminishing role of Parliament in the conduct of national affairs is broader than what has been highlighted by the Commission in the above passage. In the context of coalition politics, there is also increasing acceptance by political leaders of the frequent violation of democratic norms and conventions in the political decision-making process. As a result, there is a possible threat to the preservation of the cherished goals of 'Unity in Diversity', which, as mentioned by the prime minister, was an important gift to the nation from leaders like Mahatma Gandhi and Jawaharlal Nehru in the early years of the country's freedom. Some signs of the increasing divide in the national mainstream are already evident. As many as 160 districts of India are under the influence of Naxalites, and function largely outside the control of state governments. As the prime minister himself observed on another occasion:

> Naxalism is the single biggest internal security challenge ever faced by our country . . . the movement has gained in strength and now spread to over 160 districts all over the country . . . the extremists are trying to establish 'liberation zones' in core areas where they are dispensing basic state functions of administration, policing and justice.[3]

To what extent the growing power of militant movements reflects the weakness of the State is a moot question. It is a fact that in several states where lawlessness has spread in a large number of districts, the administration has been extremely weak. Political leadership has been ineffective, and there have been frequent and arbitrary transfers of senior police officers and other district officials. The duality of India is also evident in the increasing income disparities among the people, seen in the vast contrast between India's rising global economic clout, as reflected in the large number of Indians in the list of the world's billionaires, and the deteriorating conditions in its rural areas, where more than 70 per cent of its citizens live. This divide is also reflected in divisiveness at the highest levels of the government, where ministers and leaders belonging to different parties are inclined to follow their own agenda rather than pursuing a collective and shared vision for the nation's future.

In what follows I will take up some recent instances where the proceedings of Parliament, including its silences, posed serious challenges to the functioning of our democracy as a unifying force among people with a diversity of interests, identities, and outlook. Incidentally, what is said below largely reflects an eyewitness account of happenings in the Upper House of Indian Parliament, the Rajya Sabha. In many ways, the Rajya Sabha has also lost its separate identity, as what happens in this House largely reflects the positions taken by the different parties in the Lok Sabha, the House of the People. If the Lok Sabha is disrupted, so is the Rajya Sabha, and vice versa. If a bill is passed in the Lok Sabha without discussion because of disruptions or because sufficient time is not available for discussion, the Rajya Sabha is also likely to follow suit.

Taxation without Representation

In the annals of India's long and distinguished parliamentary history, the events that took place over five days, between 18 March and 22 March, during the Budget session of 2006 were perhaps unique. Over the course of these five days, a number of unexpected decisions were announced by the government regarding the business agendas of the two Houses, which were passively accepted by both the Houses. These decisions involved a major change in the established procedure for consideration of the Budget, a drastic revision in the business of the two Houses without adequate notice, and a sudden adjournment of Parliament *sine die* (followed by a reversal of this decision again a few days later). The passive and ready acceptance by Parliament, the supreme institution of India's democracy, of decisions that are contrary to well-established parliamentary conventions has serious implications for the future. It is, therefore, worth going into the events of these five days in March in some detail.

As per the usual procedure, the Budget session of Parliament for 2006 was convened by the President to meet in two parts—from 16 February to 17 March and again from 3 April to 28 April. However, on 7 March 2006, in view of the elections announced by the Election Commission in five states over the months of April and May, it was decided to have a longer interval between the two parts of the Budget session. The dates announced earlier for the two parts of the session were changed, and it was decided to hold the first session from 16 February to 22 March, and the second session from 10 May to 23 May. The first part was longer and the second part was a bit shorter than the original schedule, but on the whole, the entire Budget session was supposed to be long enough to permit the examination of the Budget as per established convention.

It will be recalled that, according to Rules 272 and 331G of the Rules of Procedure and Conduct of Business in the Rajya Sabha and the Lok Sabha respectively, it is mandatory for the demands for grants of the ministries and departments of the Government of India to be examined by the concerned standing committees of Parliament (which were set up

in 1993). The standing committees consist of members
of both Houses of Parliament. The agenda and the
meetings of the committees are conducted by a
chairperson, who is normally a senior member of one
of the Houses. The examination of the Budget grants
by these committees allows members, belonging to
both Houses and to different parties, to question the
senior representatives of the ministries or departments,
and also to hear and examine other witnesses, including
members of non-governmental organizations and
experts. The observations and recommendations of
these committees are normally unanimous and non-
partisan. The reports of these committees on matters
under their purview, including the Budget demands,
are submitted to the two Houses of Parliament for
consideration.

In order to allow the standing committees sufficient
time for careful consideration of the Budget demands,
it has also been the convention for the Houses of
Parliament to adjourn for about a fortnight between
the two parts of the Budget session. The first part of
the session is devoted to a general discussion of the
Budget by members and for the reply by the finance
minister on broader macro-economic aspects. The
reports of the standing committees on the ministries/
departments are considered in the second part of the
session followed by voting on demand for grants and
consideration of the Finance Bill for the new fiscal
year.

In 2006, as it happened, after the change in the
dates of the two parts of the Budget session were
announced on 7 March, a controversy arose about the

definition of the so-called 'office of profit'. Some members were alleged to have been appointed to such offices by state and Central governments, which is not permissible under the Constitution. One well-known member was also disqualified as a member of Parliament on these grounds by the President on the advice of the Election Commission. It was in the context of this controversy that a number of decisions were announced by the government, and were accepted by Parliament, which violated several well-established conventions and norms.

Thus, on 18 March 2006, all of a sudden the government decided to introduce a motion in the Rajya Sabha for the suspension of Rule 272 (and for a similar motion for the suspension of the relevant rule in the Lok Sabha). The motion to suspend consideration of Budget demands by the standing committees was moved and adopted without discussion in the two Houses on the same day. With the suspension of consideration by the standing committees, the ground was cleared for the adoption of the Budget as well as the Finance Bill in the first part of the session itself. This was an extraordinary and unprecedented event in a year when there was no change of government, no general election, and no internal or external emergency. And yet it was decided to rush the Budget through Parliament without proper consideration.

Rule 272 was suspended in the Rajya Sabha on 18 March and Rule 331 G was suspended in the Lok Sabha on the previous day. There was no session of Parliament on 19 March, which was a Sunday. On

Monday, 20 March, the consideration of the Budget demand for grants (or the appropriation bill), as passed by the Lok Sabha on 18 March, was listed in the revised list of business in the Rajya Sabha. The controversy on the office of profit issue had become more intense because of allegations and counter-allegations by the major parties about top party leaders holding various offices of profit under the Central and state governments and still continuing as members of Parliament. Nevertheless, the budget appropriations were considered and approved by the House on the same day. On the next day, Tuesday 21 March, the Finance Bill, i.e. the Bill to change tax laws, was listed in the revised list of business and was duly approved by a voice vote in the midst of considerable noise and disruption.

Developments in Parliament on Wednesday, 22 March, were, however, even more extraordinary and unexpected—and in some sense bizarre. Before Parliament met in the morning on that day, there was a strong rumour that the ruling coalition was considering exempting certain offices from the purview of the proposed offices of profit legislation by issuing an ordinance after the first part of the Budget session ended in the evening. The reason for this extra-ordinary move, as reported in the press, was to ensure the continuation of the Congress president in Parliament. She was also holding at the time the office of chairperson of the National Advisory Council (NAC) with Cabinet rank. Unfortunately, at the time of her appointment, the government had not taken steps to exempt this office, which could have been done easily and without any controversy.

The Opposition parties as a mark of protest decided to disrupt Parliament on 22 March, and not allow any listed business to be considered (the Union Budget had already been passed on the previous day). After an obituary reference, which lasted for about four minutes when the House met at 11.00 a.m., in view of the shouting by some members, it was decided by the chairman of the Rajya Sabha to adjourn the House for twenty minutes (from 11.10 a.m. to 11.30 a.m.). The House met as scheduled, but was again adjourned after four minutes of disruption, and was asked to meet at 1.00 p.m.[4] However, during those four minutes, more than a hundred papers, including the annual reports of public sector organizations, outcome and performance budgets, action taken reports, and the notifications issued by various departments of the government were laid on the table of the House by a dozen ministers in the midst of pandemonium. After assembling at 1.00 p.m., the House had to be adjourned for the third time without conducting any business. It was asked to re-assemble at 2.00 p.m.

The House met for the fourth time that day at 2.00 p.m. and was adjourned after two minutes for half an hour. Again there was a disruption and it was adjourned until 5.00 p.m. The House met for the sixth and last time at 5.00 p.m. This last session, which lasted for only fifteen minutes, completed all the listed business for the day, including the adoption of a legislative Bill without any discussion, in a noisy and disruptive House. This was the Delhi Special Police Establishment (Amendment) Bill, 2006. This Bill was passed by the Lok Sabha that morning and was included in the revised list of business of the Rajya Sabha in the afternoon. The motions for introduction, the clause-by-clause consideration, and the adoption of the Bill by the House were carried out by four separate voice votes in three minutes flat. After some more disruption, the national song (*Vande Mataram*) was played and the House adjourned *sine die* at 5.15 p.m.

No explanation was given in the House for the reasons why it was decided to suspend the Budget session after the first part. However, in response to questions by the media, it was explained by the government that the House had been adjourned *sine die* because the Budget had already been passed and hence there was hardly any business left to be transacted.

The end of the Budget session on 22 March was followed by a surprise announcement the next day, 23 March, by the Congress president. She decided to renounce her seat in Parliament, and seek re-election after resigning from all other government positions (including that of the chairperson of the National Advisory Council). According to media reports, in the light of this unexpected development, the government had no option but to give up its plans to issue an ordinance exempting certain offices from the purview of 'office of profit' rules.[5] In a subsequent press interview, it was announced by the concerned minister that the government would consult other parties in

Parliament and bring about appropriate legislation for consideration in due course.[6]

After four days of abrupt *sine die* adjournments, the government announced its intention of reconvening Parliament, as earlier scheduled, from 10 May to 23 May 2006. A formal notice to this effect was also issued to all members on 5 April 2006 after the necessary formalities had been completed. On 28 March 2006, members were also informed that 'notwithstanding the completion of discussion and voting on the Demands for Grants of the respective Ministries/Departments for the year 2006–07 by the Lok Sabha, it has been decided that the Department-related Parliamentary Standing Committees will examine these Demands for Grants and present their reports thereon to the respective Houses'.[7]

Thus, the standing committees were also resurrected as suddenly as they had been dispensed with—even though there was nothing left for them to consider, recommend, or approve. This move was yet another step in the direction of the diminishing role of Parliament in the conduct of the nation's affairs.

Parliament now does what the executive decides or does not decide, presumably after some behind-the-scenes consultations with selected party leaders. The events of 18–22 March, and the subsequent decision to reverse some of the unconventional decisions taken earlier, are perhaps a culmination of a process marked by ad hocism and expediency in the functioning of Parliament. Let me end this section by mentioning two other recent examples of the shrinking role that Parliament now performs. These examples, taken from two previous sessions of Parliament, are perhaps indicative of an emerging trend and the direction in which Parliament's role is now drifting. On 29 August 2005, a day before the end of the monsoon session last year, the Rajya Sabha adopted an important Bill, the Women's Succession Bill, in four minutes flat in the midst of shouting and the shutting out of any debate and discussion on the Bill. Members were not even able to hear the minister rising to introduce the Bill. The clause-by-clause consideration was also taken up without any member being able to speak or comment in the midst of a disruptive and noisy House. Then the Bill was passed by a voice vote, with most members not even being aware that the chair had asked for such a vote. Fortunately, this particular Bill was concerned with providing equal treatment of all citizens, in respect of inheritance, irrespective of gender, and it enjoyed wide public support. However, what was alarming was not the contents of the Bill, but the way in which it was passed. Based on this precedent, at least in principle, any other Bill, whatever its contents, is capable of being passed in the same way. As mentioned above, this is precisely what happened again—after only seven months—on 22 March 2006.

Similarly, in an uncanny resemblance to the procedure adopted for the passage of the budget for 2006, on 26 August 2004, Parliament had also decided to suspend the question hour and pass the regular Budget involving an expenditure of more than Rs 475,000 crore without any discussion within a few minutes. This was also the result of a backroom agreement between the leaders of the parties in the government and the Opposition, following several days of disruption of parliamentary work (because of a dispute on a sensitive but extraneous matter).

In 2004 and 2005, when the above events occurred, they had seemed unusual and somewhat alarming. However, in the light of developments that took place during the five days of March 2006, they pale into relative insignificance. During those five days, not only was the Budget passed abruptly in advance of the normal schedule, but an important Bill was also adopted without discussion or advance notice in a disrupted House. And then the session was adjourned *sine die*, only to be reconvened again!

It may be argued that the primary responsibility for the above series of events lies with a disgruntled Opposition, and not with the government. It was the Opposition that was indulging in frequent disruptions in the two Houses and the government had no option but to somehow carry on with the task of running the affairs of the nation. This contention may have some validity, but it does not resolve the issue of the complete subservience of Parliament to the will of the executive. If Bills can be passed, if Budgets can be approved, and if sessions can be adjourned abruptly, an irresponsible or autocratic government in future can easily get away with the erosion, and even the suspension, of the legitimate rights of the people. So far, with one or two possible exceptions, the country has been fortunate in having been led by leaders of integrity and democratic values, despite the ups and downs of coalition politics. However, there is no guarantee that this will continue to be so in the future.

There is also no legitimate explanation for the decision to end the Budget session well in advance of the announced schedule or to suspend the procedure for the examination of the Budget by the standing committees and then reverse these decisions arbitrarily after a couple of days. The sanctity of well-established conventions and practices deserves to be preserved rather than abandoned on grounds of expediency. This is feasible if Parliament, rather than the executive in power, is in charge of its own functioning and if the chairs of the two Houses are given adequate powers to control an unruly Opposition. Some suggestions to this effect are made in Chapter 6. It is the duty of a democratic and elected government, not only to somehow carry on with the business of governance, but also to ensure that the means adopted for doing so conform to democratic best practices and to the intent of the Constitution to make the executive accountable to the legislature rather than the other way round.

The Silences of Parliament

In addition to approving legislative proposals and other government business, the Parliament is an important forum for the discussion of public issues and public grievances through their representatives. There are regular 'question hours' for members to ask questions of their choice concerning different ministries. Ministers are responsible for answering these questions and for taking further action as necessary in the light of discussions on 'starred' questions. Time is allotted for members to make 'special mentions' on an issue of importance to their constituents, their states, and the country. A member is entitled to propose a 'short-duration' discussion on any matter of public importance. He or she can also move a resolution or a private member's Bill for discussion and approval after completing the necessary formalities for doing so.

Debate on important policy issues is exhaustive, penetrating, and highly useful (for example, on subjects such as the nuclear co-operation agreement with the United States, the Rural Employment Guarantee Act, development problems in the least developed parts of the country, and regional cooperation in South-east Asia). The issues raised during the debates also influence the course of policy formulation by the government of the day. This is an important strength of India's democracy as national policies of long-term domestic and international importance, including economic policies, are adopted after careful consideration and broad consensus across the political spectrum. This explains why national policies, once approved by Parliament after discussion, are seldom reversed despite changes of government.

However, there have been occasions when the silences of Parliament have been just as loud as the debates on foreign policy, employment, and development policy. Generally, the tolerance for deviation from established norms and propriety is most evident when the interests of the leader of the party in power are under threat or when there is a clash of interests among different parties in search of political power after elections (or an adverse judicial verdict). The most conspicuous example of such silences was, of course, during the period of the Emergency in 1975–77 when violations of established laws and administrative norms were either tolerated or approved through legislative amendments, including Constitutional amendments.

Fortunately for India's democracy, such occasions have been relatively infrequent. The power of Parliament to alter the fundamental rights of the people and the 'basic structure' of the Constitution has also been declared invalid by the Supreme Court of India as early as 1973 (during the hearing on the famous *Kesavananda* case). It will be recalled that the verdict of the Supreme Court in this case was challenged in 1975 by the government after the imposition of the Emergency. It was argued that Parliament was 'supreme' and represented the sovereign will of the people. As such, if the people's representatives in Parliament decided to change a particular law to curb individual freedom or to limit the scope of judicial scrutiny, the judiciary had no right to question whether it was Constitutional or not. After listening to the persuasive arguments of legal luminaries such as Nani Palkhivala, the Chief Justice of India decided to dissolve the Bench, and the 'basic structure' doctrine was reaffirmed as an unalienable feature of our Constitution.

The 'basic structure' doctrine has not been challenged or compromised by any party or parties in power after 1975. However, in recent years, the silences of Parliament have become more frequent on several issues of public interest. New state governments have been sworn in even though they did not have a majority in the legislatures. Ordinances have been issued by governments without adequate cause, and prosecution of criminal offenders has been deferred to protect the political interests of some parties or powerful leaders. On such issues of paramount national importance, Parliament has maintained a silence or has given its approval *post facto* under the Constitution in case such approval was required (for example, for imposition of President's Rule in Bihar in 2005 by ordinance, which was later found to be un-Constitutional by the Supreme Court).

Again, fortunately for India, these cases have been the exception, and despite the silences and tolerance of Parliament, the wrong decisions taken by Constitutional authorities have generally been reversed later after judicial scrutiny. However, some unhealthy precedents have been set, and it cannot be taken for granted that these will not be repeated in the future. It is useful to remind ourselves of some of the recent cases where Parliament did not play its part in holding the executive accountable for its actions. The aggrieved persons or parties needed to approach the judiciary for redressal of their grievances.

In this connection, developments in the state of Bihar after regular state elections were completed in February 2005 are of particular interest. It will be recalled that the electoral verdict in this case was fractured and that no party or combination of parties had a clear majority. This included the ruling Rashtriya Janata Dal (RJD), which had been in power for several years. After considering various options, the then Governor of the state was pleased to recommend the imposition of President's Rule without dissolving the assembly. However, after patiently waiting for three months, all of a sudden and without any notice or discussion with the various political parties, on 23 May 2005, he felt compelled to recommend that the assembly should be dissolved immediately. The Union Cabinet considered it appropriate to meet late at night and advise the President, who was on a state visit to Moscow, to approve the Governor's recommendation during the course of the night itself. The reason for this great urgency three months after the election was not made clear, although it was claimed by the Governor later that this decision had become unavoidable because 'horse-trading' among legislators was taking place. The Governor and the Government of India, therefore, considered it necessary to dissolve the assembly to prevent unethical behaviour on the part of the legislators. According to media reports and other available evidence, the real reason for the hasty action was that legislators belonging to some minority parties had decided, after waiting for three months, to join a coalition of other parties that were opposed to the RJD. As it happened, the RJD was a member of the ruling coalition at the Centre with a number of ministers in the Central Cabinet. The Centre, therefore, had no option but to take the midnight decision to prevent another coalition of parties from taking office in Bihar.

The Opposition parties in the state were naturally upset by the Centre's decision, and some of the affected legislators decided to file a case against the decision of the Government of India. In defence of its case, an affidavit was filed by the Central government in the Supreme Court. In its affidavit, the government argued that 'the Court is not to inquire—it is not concerned with whether any advice was tendered by any minister or Council of Ministers to the President, and if so, what was that advice. That is a matter between the President and his Council of Ministers.' In other words, according to the government, the Council of Ministers could advise the President to pass any order (irrespective of its merits); the President had no option but to accept that advice under the Constitution; and the Supreme Court had no right to examine whether the action of the executive was legal or not!

After hearing the arguments, in October 2005, the Supreme Court gave a summary verdict declaring the action of the government to dissolve the Bihar assembly as 'un-Constitutional' and unreasonable. The Court, however, did not order the revival of the old assembly as fresh elections had already been announced by the Election Commission and were scheduled to take place after a few days. The Court's verdict caused considerable public embarrassment to the government since the decision to dissolve the assembly had been taken by the President at very short notice on the advice of the Union Cabinet. In the light of the Supreme Court verdict, the Governor of Bihar tendered his resignation. And that was the end of the matter so far as the government was concerned.

When the above events were taking place, Parliament was in recess. The monsoon session of Parliament was reconvened in the last week of July 2005. As per the provisions of the Constitution, the ordinance to dissolve the state assembly had to be formally approved by Parliament. The government moved a Bill to that effect, which was duly approved. Interestingly, after the Supreme Court verdict in October 2005, declaring that the action to dissolve the state assembly was un-Constitutional, some parties in Parliament put forward the view that the Supreme Court in its judgment had exceeded its brief since the ordinance had already been approved by the Parliament of India! Subsequently, in November 2005, after fresh elections were held, a new coalition government was formed by the parties that had earlier been denied the right to test their majority on the floor of the assembly.

An even more blatant example of the transgression of well-established Constitutional conventions by the Governor of a state occurred in March 2005 in the state of Jharkhand. After the elections, in Jharkhand also, there was no clear majority among the pre-election allies. However, the Opposition parties were able to persuade some other elected members to join them. They were thus able to demonstrate their majority to the Governor (with forty-one members in a House of eighty members). However, in his wisdom, the Governor decided to swear in a government headed by a member of the Union Cabinet, who did not seem to have a clear majority. He was also given a number of days to prove his majority on the floor of the House. The Opposition parties that claimed to have a majority, were extremely upset by this decision of the Governor and filed a writ petition in the Supreme Court challenging the decision. On 9 March 2005, the Court passed an order that *inter alia* gave directions to the Speaker to extend the state assembly session by a day and to conduct a floor test between the contending political alliances. In the light of the Supreme Court's decision, the earlier government formed by the Union minister decided to tender its resignation on the advice of the Central government. An alternative government was then formed by a combination of other parties, which was able to prove its majority on the floor of the House.

The directions of the Supreme Court to the Speaker of the Jharkhand assembly raised a legal storm, as these were interpreted by several experts as intruding into an area that was within the jurisdiction of the legislature. This view was also endorsed by an Emergent Conference of the Presiding Officers of Legislative Bodies of India, which was convened at short notice on 20 March 2005 to deliberate on the Constitutional issues arising from the verdict of the Supreme Court. The presiding officers expressed their concern in no uncertain terms over 'such orders passed by the courts repeatedly which tend to disturb the delicate balance of power between Judiciary and Legislature and appear to be a transgression into the independence of the Parliamentary System of our Country'.

In Parliament, there was no disapproval of the undemocratic actions of the Governor. The concern expressed by presiding officers of the legislative bodies was not about the actions of the Governor. It was about the Supreme Court transgressing its jurisdiction in giving directions to the legislature for impartially carrying out the Constitutional provisions in respect of the formation of the government.

The role of state legislatures in defending the provisions of the Constitution, including the procedure for the approval of state Budgets, has become even more perfunctory than that of Parliament. In some states, the Budget sessions are now held for a few days only, and Budgets are passed practically without any discussion. The same is the case in regard to the approval of new laws or legislative amendments proposed by the government. Part of the reason for this state of affairs is the unbridled power of the Opposition to disrupt the House and the pressures of coalition politics. The greater the chaos generated when the House is in session, the greater the publicity. Such publicity is considered to be a major gain for parties, particularly small parties, outside the ruling coalition.

Coalitions and Parliament

There has been a fundamental change in India's democratic politics. This is that multi-party coalitions which include post-electoral allies, are now the norm at the Centre as well as in several states of the Union. This development is accepted by all political parties, including the Congress party which was in denial earlier. However, the implications of this important change in electoral reality for the effective governance of the country have not yet been fully appreciated.

The major implication is simply that, unlike the pre-1989 period when governments were expected to be in office for their full term of five years (except under very exceptional circumstances), today the normal expectation is that the government may fall at any time. This may happen if, for whatever reasons, one or more of its supporting parties with a relatively small strength in Parliament (of, say, 10 per cent of members in the Lok Sabha) withdraws support. Since 1989, India has undergone as many as six general elections and multiple coalitions have ruled the country. There have been seven prime ministers, five of whom had tenures ranging from a few days to about one year. Prior to 1989, in the first forty-one years of independence, six prime ministers ruled the country, of whom only three had tenures of less than five years.

The frequency of elections and the expectation that the tenure of a new government and a new Lok Sabha may be short, has had several unintended consequences for the functioning of Parliament and other vital pillars of India's democracy. The power of the leader of a party over its members in Parliament is supreme and unquestioned, and what happens in Parliament now is largely determined by the political interests of different parties rather than by the intrinsic merits or demerits of actions taken by the executive. Most of the smaller parties have a narrow social base, but their leaders enjoy considerable political power in view of their ability to swing relatively small numbers of votes in favour of another party, particularly in marginal seats. The frequent splits in parties, and the tendency among smaller party formations to destabilize governments, have important behavioural implications for coalitions that come to power after elections.

In order to prevent the destabilization of a government by splitting a party that is a part of the ruling coalition and to prevent cross-voting during the Rajya Sabha elections, it will be recalled that two important legislative changes were adopted by Parliament in April 2003. The first amendment was that any elected member (or a group of members) who decided to leave his or her party would have to seek fresh election. The second amendment (pertaining to election to the Rajya Sabha) replaced secret voting by an open-voting process by members of legislatures. This amendment was designed to prevent cross-voting so that members who did not vote for their party's candidates could be removed from their party for 'indiscipline'. The domicile requirement of candidates for election to the Rajya Sabha was also removed.

On the face of it, these amendments seem sensible because they are designed to reduce instability and corruption among the members of a party. However, in reality, the effect has been to strengthen the powers of party leaders over their members. The solution adopted, with multi-party consensus, is in fact a lot worse than the disease. While members have no right to defect, the leader of a small party is free to create instability by forcing all members of the party to leave the coalition, even if the majority of the members do not agree with that decision. Similarly, nomination to the Rajya Sabha has become the sole prerogative of the leader of a party (and a few persons who enjoy his confidence). Bribery or the funding of parties in exchange for nomination to the Rajya Sabha has also not been curbed. Indeed, in the long run, the new amendment may encourage institutionalized corruption in the nomination process.

While Parliament sessions are held frequently and vast quantities of papers containing information on the working of ministries are placed before it, the events of March 2006 have established beyond reasonable doubt that Parliament has practically no role in holding the government accountable for its performance or even deciding when and for how long it will meet to conduct its business. It is now a regular practice for government business or legislative proposals that require parliamentary approval to be approved without much debate and within a few minutes towards the end of the day when only a few members, including those from the parties in power, are present.

There was a time when assurances given by ministers on the floor of Parliament had a ring of credibility to them. Unlike other commitments, those made in the two Houses were supposed to be translated into reality if only for the fear of attracting motions of breach of privilege. This is no longer the case. Assurances in Parliament are now just like any other assurance, meant to be bypassed or forgotten without explanation. Hundreds of assurances, some of them made more than a decade ago, are still pending. With the higher turnover of ministers, nobody takes any personal responsibility for assurances given by previous ministers.

Another consequence of the expectation that a particular multi-party coalition, which is dependent on the support of a large number of other parties, may not last long is the politicization of civil administration at the Centre, states, and districts. Increasingly, with the possibility of only a short duration in ministerial offices, the political leadership, with a few honourable exceptions, is inclined to give preference to its party's political, sectional and financial objectives rather than the larger public interest.

The purpose of highlighting the wider implications of multi-party coalitions in the functioning of Parliament and in other areas of governance is not to undermine the legitimacy of coalitions in a democracy. As in several other countries, coalitions are—from time to time—unavoidable in a parliamentary system of government, or for that matter in a presidential system with a separate legislature. The parliamentary system of government, as I will elaborate in a later chapter, is also the most viable and the best for India.

At the same time, it has to be recognized that if disparate multi-party coalitions have become a regular feature of our governance system, then certain changes in parliamentary procedures are also essential, such as those pertaining to the role of small parties and the system for enforcing accountability of the executive for its decisions. This is particularly important in a country that is characterized by widespread poverty, disparity, and deprivation among its people. It is possible that in other more developed and advanced democratic countries, unstable governments with low probability of survival may not cause as much damage to the larger public interest as may happen in a developing and predominantly rural society like that of India.

It also has to be recognized that the emergence of coalitions as a regular form of government was not fully foreseen at the time that our Constitution and the rules of parliamentary procedures were adopted after considerable debate. In the light of emerging requirements and experience, so far India has carried out more than a hundred amendments in its original Constitution and adopted several changes to its electoral and legislative procedures. If some more amendments are now necessary to accommodate the realities of coalition governments as a regular feature of our democracy, these must be undertaken sooner rather than later.

References

1. Speech by the Prime Minister of India to mark the Ram Nath Goenka Awards for Excellence in Journalism on 12 April 2006, as reported in the *Indian Express*, New Delhi, 13 April 2006.

2. *Report of the National Commission to Review the Working of the Constitution* (2002), Government of India, New Delhi, p. 105.

3. *Second Meeting of Standing Committee of Chief Ministers on Naxalism*, Concluding Remarks by the Prime Minister, as reported in the *Economic Times*, New Delhi, 14 April 2006.

4. *Proceedings of the Meeting of the Rajya Sabha held on 22 March 2006*, Parliament of India, New Delhi.

5. *Times of India*, New Delhi, 24 March 2006.

6. *Indian Express*, New Delhi, 26 March 2006.

7. *Parliamentary Bulletin*, Rajya Sabha, Parliament of India, New Delhi, 28 March 2006.

FIVE

The Executive and the Judiciary

According to Article 75 of the Constitution of India, 'The Council of Ministers shall be collectively responsible to the House of the People.' However, as we have seen in the previous chapter, the responsibility of the Council of Ministers to the House of the People or the Parliament of India is largely *pro forma*. As the events of the five days in March 2006, from 18 March to 22 March, abundantly demonstrated, as long as a government can command the support of a majority of members belonging to one or more parties, it is the will of the government that prevails in Parliament rather than the other way round. Parliament may be convened to meet during a specified period in the future, but it may be abruptly adjourned *sine die* without any explanation if the government so decides; the decision to adjourn *sine die* may also be reversed a few days later after Parliament has actually adjourned; the Budget and the Finance Bill may be approved by voice votes at a day's notice; and a legislative Bill may be passed in the midst of a disrupted House without any discussion.

In the era of coalition governments consisting of parties with different political agendas, the notion of the collective responsibility of the Council of Ministers has also suffered. Ministers are inclined to push forward their own interests or party priorities without informing the Cabinet or even the prime minister as head of the Council of Ministers. The erosion of collective responsibility has been accompanied by a process of politicization of the permanent civil services. The old notion that the civil services should render impartial and apolitical advice to the ministers has been abandoned to a large extent. With unlimited powers of transfers and appointments in the hands of ministers, civil servants are fully at their mercy. Whenever a new government or a new minister comes into office—even after a few months—there is likely to be a reshuffle of civil servants according to the political preferences of the key ministers belonging to different parties.

Fortunately, despite the emergence of coalition politics and its impact on administration, the judiciary continues to be the final arbiter of the legality or otherwise of decisions taken by the executive either on its own or with the approval of Parliament, as required. In the light of the Supreme Court's 1973 decision (in the famous *Kesavananda* case), which confirmed that the 'basic structure' of the Constitution was sacrosanct, the judiciary continues to have the ultimate power to interpret the Constitution and its intent.

While there is common agreement among all the organs of the state, i.e. the legislature, the executive, and the judiciary, on their respective powers and jurisdictions, from time to time a dispute arises about whether the judiciary has exceeded its powers in issuing directions to the other branches of the government in the light of its own interpretation of the provisions of the Constitution. The dispute about the judiciary having exceeded its powers becomes intense when the executive branch at the Centre or in the states takes a decision that is apparently in favour of some parties at the expense of other parties. Irrespective of the intrinsic merits or otherwise of the decisions taken in such situations, an appeal to the courts by aggrieved parties and legislators becomes unavoidable. This is precisely what happened after the indecisive electoral verdicts in three states, i.e. Goa, Jharkhand, and Bihar in early 2005. Neither the Governors of these states (who had the final powers to appoint a government) nor the presiding officers of the legislatures (who had the power to conduct the proceedings of the House to test the majority) were considered to be impartial in their decisions. The aggrieved legislators went to the Court, and the Court issued certain interim directions to the executive and/ or the legislature as per its interpretation of the Constitution. The directions of the Court, in turn, led to protests by members of the new government as well as the presiding officers about the Court having exceeded its jurisdiction in issuing such directions.

It is no accident that in India's democratic history, the political pressure to limit the powers of the judiciary and declare Parliament as being 'supreme' and representative of the will of the 'people of India' is the strongest when a coalition government of parties with varying agendas is in power, or when the political survival of the undisputed leader of the majority party is threatened (as, for example, was the case in 1975 when the Emergency was imposed). In these circumstances, political survival becomes more important than the legal merits or demerits of a case.

The erosion in the Constitutional principle of collective responsibility, the politicization of the bureaucracy, and the dispute about the separation of powers between the judiciary and the executive (or legislature) have important implications for the working of India's political system and its institutions. Some of these implications are discussed below.

The Principle of Collective Responsibility

In the parliamentary system of government, unlike the presidential system, all members of the Cabinet are members of the legislature (the Parliament at the federal level and the state assemblies at the state level). The prime minister is elected to head the government by the party that has won majority (or is selected by consensus among the parties in a coalition), and is supposed to be 'first among equals'. The prime minister in turn selects the members of the Cabinet and assigns them to different ministries and departments of the government as ministers or ministers of state. The prime minister is also free to create new ministries and departments or to merge and change the items of business assigned to different ministries. In the formation of new governments, depending on their personal standing in the party and the extent of political power they enjoy, prime ministers are free to act on their own or they may need to consult the leader of their party and its coalition partners.

Once the decisions concerning the composition of the Council of Ministers have been made and communicated to the President, these decisions are final. The Cabinet is then supposed to be collectively responsible to Parliament or the legislatures. All policy decisions taken by individual ministries, irrespective of who heads them, and all laws or amendments to existing laws have to be approved by the Cabinet as a whole before they are introduced in Parliament. Similarly, all important administrative decisions, including appointments, are supposed to be put up to the Cabinet or to a designated committee of the Cabinet after appropriate inter-ministerial consultations. In case there is any disagreement among the ministries, such a disagreement has to be explicitly brought before the Cabinet or the concerned committee of the Cabinet for discussion and resolution. All Cabinet decisions, once approved, are unanimous and the Cabinet is collectively responsible for them.

The principle of collective responsibility of the Cabinet has some important Constitutional implications for the conduct of individual ministers, however powerful they may be in their own parties. First, no major policy or administrative decision should be taken without appropriate inter-ministerial consultations and the approval of the prime minister. Second, all such decisions must represent a consensus among members of the Cabinet or its committees, whether they are directly concerned with the subject under consideration or not. Third, all members of the Cabinet are jointly and collectively responsible for the performance of the government in Parliament (and thus indirectly to the people), irrespective of the particular ministry to which a particular item of business has been allotted.

An important corollary of the principle of collective responsibility is that no individual minister can be formally held accountable for the failure of a ministry to implement a decision or a programme announced by the government. Thus, to take an extreme example, the government can declare war or sign a peace or border treaty, which may later be considered to be unwarranted or badly implemented. An individual minister, however, cannot be held responsible for the wrong decision or failure in implementation. The Council of Ministers as a whole—irrespective of any internal dissension and disagreement—would have to rise in defence of the minister. The prime minister or the leader of the party is, of course, free to ask the minister to resign or remove him or her. However, so far as the public or Parliament is concerned, he or she has no formal individual responsibility and accountability for implementing the decisions taken on behalf of the government. An individual minister cannot be censured or suspended by Parliament for any policy or administrative decision taken by his or her ministry with the approval of the Cabinet. Questions may be asked, calling attention motions may be moved and even cases may be filed in courts for impropriety or corruption, but the person can continue in office as long as the prime minister wishes him to and the party in power enjoys a majority in the House.

Against the above background, it is not surprising that successive governments and ministers, since Independence, have announced grand plans for removing poverty, achieving full employment, and providing essential services to the people. And yet India, despite all the recent growth and shine, remains one of the poorest countries in the world with the highest number of poor persons, who enjoy the right to vote and elect their government. Programmes aimed at removing poverty and providing services to the poor have also been the principal items on the economic agenda of every political party at the time of elections. The instrumentalities and specific policies proposed to be adopted, if voted to power, have varied from one party to another, but the anti-poverty objective has been the same. In view of this, it is surprising that, despite the increasing frequency of elections and the different combinations of parties that have formed governments in recent years, the public delivery system has continued to deteriorate. The poor, of course, continue to have the power to vote, and enjoy substantial electoral power in a majority of constituencies in the country. But once the elections are over, accountability for the performance of ministers is conspicuous by its absence.

While the principle of collective responsibility has effectively shielded individual ministers from being held accountable for the performance of their ministries, this principle has not prevented them from taking decisions on matters of great public importance without seeking a consensus among the coalition partners or even the formal approval of the Cabinet. There have been several such cases in the recent past. In order to appreciate the full implications of the erosion of the principle of collective responsibility, which shields ministers from taking individual responsibility, let us consider two recent cases.

In March 2004, when the National Democratic Alliance (NDA) coalition was in power, the then minister in charge of higher education announced the decision of his ministry to drastically reduce the financial autonomy enjoyed by the Indian Institutes of Management (IIMs). This decision, which was taken by the minister without any reference or endorsement of the Cabinet, would have had major implications for the viability of the IIMs, which had contributed significantly to improving corporate governance and competitiveness. The decision of the ministry led to widespread protests by the IIMs and other educational institutions. The ministry then announced that, in order to ensure the financial viability of the IIMs, the government would provide adequate direct subsidy to cover the difference between the cost of providing an education and the amount that the IIMs were going to be allowed to charge by way of fees. In other words, the government was prepared to subsidize even those students who could afford to pay higher fees in order to impose 'price controls' on the IIMs! This latter decision was also announced without the approval of the Cabinet or the ministry responsible for the Budget (i.e. the Ministry of Finance).

However, before the above decision could be implemented, there was a change in government and a new coalition came to power. In May 2004, the new minister decided to reverse the earlier decision. This was widely welcomed by the IIMs as well as other educational institutions. Thus, two diametrically opposite decisions with serious implications for the future of higher education in India were announced by the same ministry within a space of two months under two different ministers. These decisions reflected their policy preferences and were taken without adequate consultations or discussions with the Cabinet and with others concerned with the matter.

After some time, in April 2006, another major controversy erupted in the field of higher education following the announcement by the concerned minister that, in addition to reservations for Scheduled Castes and Scheduled Tribes (SCs and STs), the government had also decided to introduce quotas for Other Backward Classes (OBCs) in institutions such as the IIMs, the Indian Institutes of Technology and medical colleges. The decision to exercise the general powers available to the government to impose quotas with immediate effect was also announced without the formal prior approval of the Cabinet, and was publicly opposed by another Cabinet minister. The breakdown of the collective decision-making process in the Cabinet was widely commented upon by the media. The divided viewpoint within the Cabinet had the effect of making the entire admission policy highly uncertain for the students and the faculty of some of the best-known institutions in the country for quite some time until the policy was finally approved by the Cabinet.

Another recent controversy was in respect of the ongoing construction work on the Sardar Sarovar project by the Narmada Control Authority. In March 2006, the Narmada Bachao Andolan strongly protested against the lack of adequate progress in the rehabilitation of persons affected by the decision to raise the height of the dam. The protest attracted considerable public sympathy because of the decision of some of the supporters of the Andolan to go on a fast unto death. Three Cabinet ministers, including the minister in charge of the Water Resources Ministry, visited the site in order to persuade the protesters to break their fast. After a brief visit to assess the progress of work on rehabilitation, but without adequate consultation with the concerned state governments or the Union Cabinet, the ministers announced their preference for stopping the construction work to raise the height of the dam. Since this was a major decision, which would have adversely affected the availability of power and water in several states, the concerned minister decided to refer the matter to the prime minister. At the same time, the chief minister of one of the major states also decided to go on a fast to voice his protest against the views expressed by the Union minister. Fortunately for the Union government, the matter was already scheduled to come up for a hearing before the Supreme Court the next day. The Court had earlier approved the proposal to raise the height of the dam, subject to the time-bound rehabilitation of the affected persons. The Supreme Court gave the necessary directions to the Centre and the concerned state governments, which helped diffuse the imminent crisis.

These and similar other cases, where particular ministers have decided to announce important government decisions on their own, have now become matters of considerable public concern. No one really knows what the collective view of the government is on matters of public importance and the validity of pronouncements by individual ministers on controversial issues. The confusion has been further compounded by the disparate ideologies of the constituent parties in several recent coalitions and by open political differences among members of the same Cabinet at the Centre as well as in the states. There have also been cases where ministers in office have publicly expressed their disagreement with important Cabinet decisions (for example, in respect of the Union government's decision to dissolve the state assembly of Bihar in 2005). Despite their disagreement with a formal Cabinet decision, contrary to parliamentary norms in mature democracies, the concerned ministers did not resign as members of the Union Cabinet.

For the future governance of the country, an important issue that requires consideration is: if, on the one hand, the Cabinet cannot be assumed to be collectively responsible for ministerial pronouncements and, on the other hand, ministers cannot be held individually responsible, then who should take responsibility for the actions taken or not taken on behalf of the government? This question has become even more pertinent in the light of the diminishing role of Parliament in enforcing the accountability of the Council of Ministers (see Chapter 4). As a commentator has rightly observed:

> Cabinet ministers have repeatedly gone off at a
> policy tangent and given the impression no one can
> control them . . . these ministers also threatened,
> sometimes implicitly, sometimes publicly, that their
> biggest loyalties lay outside the government and the
> party . . . Distancing the PMO [Prime Minster's
> Office] and the party from unruly senior members
> and/or their statements cannot control the damage.
> It simply reinforces the perception of weak authority.
> And it provokes voters to ask: who's in charge?[1]

The answer to this question must be found at the
political level through consensus among all parties
and their constituents. In the era of coalitions, ministers
have to be held *individually* accountable for their
actions. Parliament also has to become more assertive
in enforcing collective accountability for the aggregate
performance of its Council of Ministers. We will
return to these issues in the next chapter on political
reforms.

The Politicization of Administration

A great deal has been written on the atrophy, non-
accountability, corruption and inaptitude of the Indian
administrative system (Ray 2001).[2] In addition to
academics, outside observers, international agencies
and the general public, a number of civil servants
have also written their memoirs or recounted their
experiences after their retirement from the highest
offices of the State. There is now almost complete
unanimity that, despite having some of the best and
brightest persons in the civil services, the system as a
whole has become non-functional, and that there is

very little possibility of reforming it. This situation has arisen despite a great deal of trying, including efforts made at different levels by distinguished committees, commissions, associations and public-spirited persons. These efforts have come to naught because the system is dominated by internal conflicts of interest (for example, among separate trade unions for different classes of government employees), political interference, outdated statutory provisions, complicated seniority-bound procedures, fiscal stringency, and the proliferation of administrative agencies that operate at cross purposes without any clear division of work.

This was not always so. Indeed, for many years after Independence, India's civil services were regarded as exemplary among developing nations. Under India's system of public administration, there was supposed to be a clear division of roles between the permanent civil service and the political leadership. The bureaucracy was subordinate to the elected politicians, who were chosen by the prime minister at the Centre (and by the chief ministers in the states) to head different ministries and departments. The government's priorities and its work programme were set by the elected politicians, and the bureaucracy was supposed to ensure that this programme was implemented according to the laws in force and in line with approved administrative procedures. While implementing the programmes set by the Cabinet and the ministers, bureaucrats were expected to act without fear or favour and to ensure that the benefits of the programmes flowed to the people regardless of their political affiliations. While the elected politicians were free to overrule the advice rendered by civil servants, the advisory functions of the bureaucracy were expected to be performed without regard to their impact on the private interests of politicians and the party in power.

Over the years, slowly but surely, the role of the bureaucracy has unfortunately been seriously compromised. Thus, according to the recent report of the National Commission set up to review the working of the Constitution:

> Arbitrary and questionable methods of appointments, promotions and transfers of officers by political superiors also led to corrosion of the moral basis of its independence. It has strengthened the temptation in services to collusive practices with politicians to avoid the inconvenience of transfers and for officers to gain advantages by ingratiating themselves to political masters. They would do the politicians' biddings rather than adhere to rules. Lest the situation becomes more vicious, it is necessary that a better arrangement be conceived under the Constitution.[3]

In recent years, the politicization of the bureaucracy has gathered further momentum as a result of governments with short tenures pursuing their private or party interests in the guise of promoting the larger public good. Any party that comes to power is inclined to appoint favoured bureaucrats in sensitive positions who are expected to carry out the wishes of its party leaders, irrespective of their merits or legality. If a bureaucrat does not comply, he or she is likely to be transferred immediately to another position in another location. According to a study, in one year alone, in the state of Uttar Pradesh (when there was a six-monthly rotation of the government headed by the leaders of the two parties in a coalition, the BJP and the BSP), there were 1,000 transfers among the members of the elite Indian Administrative Service (IAS) and the Indian Police Service (IPS). Under one head of government, transfers of officers, including those from the IAS and the IPS, ran at an average of seven per day. Under the second head of government, who took office after the expiry of six months, transfers at different levels rose to sixteen per day! Over half the corps of IAS officers, at the top of the official hierarchy, were transferred within twelve months of posting.[4]

The deleterious effects of frequent transfers on the morale and effectiveness of top civil servants have been substantial. The costs to the country in terms of loss of quality of administration have also been significant. Administration has become increasingly weak and arbitrary since there is no time available to a newly appointed civil servant to acquire even the minimum knowledge necessary for an effective discharge of functions. Incompetence at the top leads to acts of passive resistance and delays by subordinates. Corruption becomes unavoidable, both to avoid transfers as well as to secure remunerative postings by corrupt officials.

As a result of the above developments, the administrative system, with multiple agencies involved at different levels in implementing government programmes, has now largely become ineffective and non-responsive. The common experience of all citizens who have to deal with a government agency for any purpose, large and small, is that of insuperable problems and delays. There is also a large diversion of funds from the intended purposes to bureaucrats, politicians, and middlemen at various levels of the administrative hierarchy. Thus, in a memorable and widely quoted observation, after visiting some important development programmes, Prime Minister Rajiv Gandhi had pointed out that: 'Out of Rs 100 crore allocated to an anti-poverty project, I know that only Rs 15 crore reaches the people. The remainder is gobbled up by middlemen, power brokers, contractors and the corrupt.'[5]

A host of recommendations for improving the system have been made by numerous high-powered committees. However, the general view among experts and experienced civil servants now seems to be that the reform of the system is not feasible. This is not because the country does not know what to do but because of political resistance to the reform of the civil service. Thus, a former Cabinet Secretary, who has recently written his memoirs—and who should know—has pointed out that:

> Politics having become the most lucrative business in the country, with few checks and controls, there is a compulsion for the minister or political leader to attempt to coerce civil servants to collude with him for mutual benefit . . . The service rules and procedures have been progressively adapted to facilitate this process.[6]

Again, as is the case in respect to effects of corruption (see Chapter 3), the worst sufferers of the politicization of administration are the poor because of their dependence on public services and government programmes for various facilities, such as subsidized food and health services. Unfortunately, the poor also face the maximum degree of indifference and harassment from government staff in securing access to their entitlements. Thus, a survey by the Public Affairs Centre found that, in Delhi, the average slum dweller needed to make six trips to a government agency to resolve a problem, and that in only 6 per cent of the cases was his or her problem attended to. People from other households had to make four trips, and in their case the rate of success was substantially higher but still only 27 per cent.[7]

The insensitivity of the administrative system to the needs of the poor, even to the urgent necessity of preventing starvation, has been confirmed by first-hand surveys and several reports by journalists and non-governmental organizations. One such survey revealed that in remote villages children were dying of hunger despite the country's godowns bursting at the seams with public stocks of food, and despite more than Rs 40,000 crore that the Central government had allocated for expenditure on anti-poverty schemes. On further investigation, it was found that 'the vast network of officials set up to take care of the interests of the poor was in denial'.[8] Similarly, it was found that many villages were without water even after the rains because the water channels and tanks had fallen into disuse as the government had announced its intention of providing piped water out of taps. While some construction work had been started to provide tap water, the project was, however, left unfinished. As a result, the villagers had access to neither tap water nor old-style tanks or wells within a reasonable distance.

The indifference of the administrative system towards the poor in providing them with their legitimate entitlements is the principal reason for the increasing disparities between urban and rural areas as well as the widening in income levels of different classes of citizens. The poor and the unemployed are more dependent on the government than is the case with other sections of the people, particularly those who are employed in the organized sector and/or have access to services provided by other non-governmental sources.

In addition to control over the services provided by the government, another fertile area for reaping political benefits is the control over public sector enterprises (see Chapter 2). Many crucial sectors of the economy are dominated by public enterprises, for example, railways, airports, public transport, oil, steel, coal, banking and insurance. For nearly four decades after Independence, many of these sectors were also characterized by widespread controls and shortages. The powers of issuing licences and allocating distribution channels for goods and services to beneficiaries (e.g. petrol pumps) were enjoyed by political authorities in charge of different ministries.

Over the last two decades, most of the controls over the economy have been removed and shortages of various kinds have also largely disappeared because of the abolition of import quotas, reduction in monopolies, and entry of new producers. Nevertheless, given the large role of public enterprises in the economy, the control of such enterprises still confers substantial powers to ministers-in-charge in dispensing political patronage to the suppliers and buyers of various kinds of goods and services. In theory, the administrative power over these enterprises is expected to be exercised by their management under the overall supervision of the boards of directors. In practice, however, the ministries exercise substantial visible and invisible control over their functioning. For example, the boards are appointed by the ministries, and there are representatives of ministries on every board to guide its deliberations. The chairman and the managing directors are also appointed by the government, formally on the advice of an autonomous Public Enterprises Selection Board (PESB). However, an enterprising minister can have considerable say in the matter of appointments by delaying action, or by not acting on the PESB recommendations, or by asking for a fresh panel on some ground or the other. Large contracts for new projects also require ministerial approval after all other technical and procedural formalities have been completed. Ministries have the final say on all policy matters, for example, pricing policy or financial policy, including the issue of additional shares to the public.

The greatest impact of political control and lack of autonomy on the management of public enterprises has been on their profitability and return on capital employed. Managers of public enterprises have virtually no flexibility in respect of operational or policy issues concerning their companies, such as shifting of branches, choice of delivery outlets, changing of the product mix, pricing of products, redeployment of staff, raising fresh capital, corporate planning, and so on. While opportunities foregone and inefficient use of resources often impose heavy costs on public enterprises (and on the government in those cases where direct subsidies are provided to such enterprises in the Budget), the social returns and benefits to the public are generally meagre. The state of rural infrastructure and public services (such as health and sanitation) continues to be appalling by any standard. To deliver one rupee of welfare benefit or food subsidy to the poor (for example, employment on rural works or food grains), the costs incurred by public enterprises and the government may amount to three or four rupees—or even more due to diversion, staff salaries, and corruption. As multiple government agencies and ministries at different levels at the Centre and the states are involved in programming and implementation, no one can be held directly responsible for diversions or other corrupt practices.

Separation of Powers

Earlier, a reference was made to the disputes that arise from time to time about the relative boundaries of the powers and jurisdictions of the three organs of the State, namely, the legislature, the executive, and the judiciary. It was also noted that such disputes tend to become more frequent when the political interests of the leading parties in a coalition or their leaders are under threat. While the Constitution broadly defines the jurisdiction and responsibility of each organ of the State, in disputed cases involving the legislative or the executive branch, the final-level decision is left to the judgment of the judicial branch.

In a parliamentary system of government, members of legislatures as well as of the Cabinet are directly, and in some cases indirectly, elected by the people. Members of the judiciary, on the other hand, are unelected and do not necessarily represent the 'will of the people'. The right to pass legislation belongs to the legislature, while the executive functions are supposed to be carried out under the direction of the Council of Ministers. In cases of dispute over the jurisdictional boundaries of the three branches of the State, the legislature can, with some justification, argue that it is the supreme law-making body and that the courts should not pass verdicts that have the effect of changing the legal position as approved by the representatives of the people. In defence of this position, it can be further pointed out that the courts can also be wrong. Thus, some court rulings in the past were wrong in law and had to be overturned by subsequent rulings by a higher court or a larger bench of the Supreme Court. No court, not even the Supreme Court, therefore, can be considered to be infallible.

It is true that, *prima facie*, some of the past Constitutional judgments were indeed protective of private interests. For example, soon after Independence, in 1951, several court rulings overturned land reform measures as being violative of the fundamental rights of landowners. The government, led by Jawaharlal

Nehru, had to amend the Constitution to implement land reforms, which were considered vital for the country's economic and social progress. Similarly, in 1970, the Supreme Court had also ruled against the nationalization of banks undertaken by Mrs Indira Gandhi's government. Special legislation had to be passed by Parliament to make bank nationalization possible. A number of other instances could be cited where the judgment of the Supreme Court and other courts was not in line with popular expectations.

While all these arguments have some validity, keeping in view the recent political developments at the Centre and in the states, I am firmly of the view that, on balance, the long-term interests of the public and the ordinary citizen are safer when the Supreme Court continues to be the watchdog of India's democratic conventions and the final arbiter of the Constitutional validity of any law or action approved by the legislature or the government of the day.[9] This view, I must emphasize, is not meant to detract from the merits of the parliamentary system of government in unifying India and giving us the freedoms that we as the people cherish.

At the same time, we have to recognize that during a period of frequent changes in government and a diminution in the role of legislatures, it is not prudent or politic for the ordinary citizen of India to confer supremacy on legislatures without accountability. The legality of executive action must continue to be subject to judicial scrutiny, however high the level at which such decisions were taken. As pointed out in the previous section, in recent years

ministries have become increasingly subject to the
unilateral policy preferences of individual ministers
who happen to be in office at a particular point of
time. There is seldom any worthwhile public debate
or constructive dialogue on matters of long-term
public importance. The issue here is not whether the
decision taken by a particular minister on behalf of
his ministry is right or wrong. The issue here is one
of long-term public interest. If a minister is able to
turn the economic or social policies of the country
one way or the other without adequate discussion and
accountability, what stops him from passing laws or
rules that have an adverse long-term impact on the
welfare of the people as a whole, or sections of the
people who are not aligned to his party?

As mentioned earlier, the Supreme Court and
other courts are not infallible, and have also given
judgments that had to be reversed in subsequent
hearings. The courts are by no means full of noble
sages, but they do provide an additional recourse for
restraining the excesses of the executive in the exercise
of the enormous powers available to it. From the
point of view of the average citizen, the great advantage
of the judicial review of decisions taken by the executive
and the legislature is that everyone, irrespective of his
or her beliefs and political affiliations, has access to
the courts. This is not the case in respect of the
executive or Parliament or state legislatures. The free
media do play a constructive role in enforcing a
degree of accountability on the part of the government,
but that by itself is not enough.

The other advantage of the judiciary being the

arbiter of the legality or otherwise of an executive or legislative decision is that, even if a particular verdict is wrong or socially unacceptable, it is subject to review and reversal. This is usually not the case with legislative or executive decisions unless the government of the day so decides. A citizen has no legal right to ask for a review of the decisions taken by the legislature or the executive, even if these are not in the public interest. The recent Right to Information Act (2005) is an important step forward in making the executive accountable to the people directly. However, in case of any unjust or partisan decisions taken by the government, the remedy would still lie with the judiciary.

Against the above background, let us consider briefly the merits of two recent cases involving electoral verdicts in Jharkhand and Bihar, which I mentioned earlier, regarding the alleged incursion of the judiciary into areas belonging to the legislature or the executive. Thus, in respect of the directions given by the Supreme Court to the Speaker of the Jharkhand assembly in March 2005, it is certainly possible to take the view that the Court went a bit too far in telling the Speaker exactly what to do (including, for example, asking for a video recording of the proceedings). However, there is very little doubt that the partisan action to swear in a government that did not have a majority, followed by efforts to prevent an alternative government from being formed by another combination of parties, was against all canons of fair play and long-standing legislative conventions. Let us suppose for the sake of argument that the Supreme Court had dismissed the case on the ground that the judiciary could not intervene in a case involving the Speaker's action in the legislature. Would the refusal of the Court to hear the case have helped the country and the average citizen in upholding the fundamental democratic rights conferred by the Constitution?

In this connection, I should mention that the Hon'ble Speaker of the Lok Sabha in his Nani Palkhivala Memorial Lecture on 12 May 2005 before the Bar Association of India raised an important and legitimate issue.[10] He rightly asked the question: What would have happened if the Supreme Court order could not be implemented by the Speaker because of the disturbances and disruption caused by the members in the House? Would the judiciary have been able to deal with the situation, or would it have filed a case of contempt against the Speaker and members of the House? In case the Court's directions could not be implemented and the Court was unable to secure the enforcement of its orders, the country would have been faced with a most difficult situation and a Constitutional deadlock.

The point is well taken. However, this does not resolve the basic issue of instituting a mechanism for protecting the democratic rights of citizens (and, for that matter, of a large body of elected members of a legislature) in the event of an unwarranted exercise of discretionary powers by the Governor, the government, or the Speaker—or a combination of them. The enforcement of the Supreme Court's orders in all democracies is ultimately the responsibility of the executive, which exercises authority over all enforcement agencies of the State. Courts themselves have no direct means of enforcing their orders, whether these orders relate to individuals, organizations, the government, or to any other entity. If the executive, with or without the approval of the legislature, decides to exceed its Constitutional authority and ignore the Supreme Court's orders, there is nothing that the Court itself can do except reiterate or revise its orders. If, because of the inaction of the executive, there is a Constitutional breakdown, the ultimate remedy lies only with the people.

In the Bihar case, a related issue that caused some legal controversy was the timing of the initial summary verdict of the Supreme Court in October 2005 without explaining the full rationale. It was argued that, even without the Court's summary judgment, state elections would have gone ahead anyway. The Court's incomplete summary verdict did not change the course of events, and gave rise to an avoidable controversy about the decision taken by the Head of State on the recommendation of the Union Cabinet. This was perhaps a reasonable view, and it would have certainly been better had the Court given its decision in full. However, this does not deflect from the main point that an important decision taken by the Union Cabinet in a hurry on the Governor's recommendation was not adequately supported by the available facts on the ground.

The legal position in the United States in respect of the separation of powers, enshrined in its Constitution for well over two centuries, is also of some relevance to India. In the United States, the head of the executive branch, the president, and his Cabinet are not members of Congress. The justices of the Supreme Court are appointed for life after being nominated by the president and after being approved by the Congress. However, once appointed, they are accountable to no other branch of the State. Their responsibility is to uphold the Constitution, which empowers them to overrule the other branches of the government. The Supreme Court is the final arbiter of the Constitutional limits of the powers of the Congress and the president.

As is the case in India, all the judges of the US Supreme Court are entitled to take their own separate views on the intent of the Constitution and vote accordingly. However, in the United States, each judge is appointed for life, and the president and the Congress have only limited powers in influencing the Court's composition during their tenures. Whenever a vacancy occurs, there is, therefore, considerable public excitement and close scrutiny of the ideology and legal credentials of the presidential nominees. Some of the famous decisions of the Supreme Court, for example in the *Roe v. Wade* verdict in 1973, which legalized abortion under certain circumstances, or the 2005 *Kelo v. New London* decision, which expanded the government's power of eminent domain (by a narrow 5–4 majority) and allowed state governments to demolish private waterfront houses, aroused considerable public controversy among different ideological groups. The *Roe* decision expanded private rights, and the *Kelo* decision severely restricted these under certain circumstances. However, while the arguments about the merits of these and other decisions have been intense, and review petitions have also been filed, no one has questioned the unfettered right of the courts to review whether the decisions taken by Congress and the state legislatures are in conformity with Constitutional provisions.

Keeping in view our own experience as well as the experience of other democracies, it is clear that a rigid demarcation of legal powers among the different branches, irrespective of the specific circumstances, is neither feasible nor desirable. By and large, under normal circumstances, it is appropriate for the different branches of the State to work in harmony and confine themselves to their primary tasks as enshrined in the Constitution. Parliament as the highest representative body should have the unquestioned authority to pass laws that it considers appropriate. The executive branch should be accountable to Parliament, and should have full administrative powers to implement laws and programmes as approved by Parliament. And the judiciary should give verdicts and settle legal disputes as per the law of the land. Most of the time, in all mature democracies, there should also be no cause for jurisdictional conflict among different organs of the State.

However, there are times when sectional interests and the 'compulsions of coalition politics' can become the primary drivers of the laws passed by Parliament and/or the administrative actions taken by the executive. Some of these laws and executive decisions may run counter to the intent of the Constitution and adversely affect the fundamental rights of the people. If the political majority in Parliament is fragmented, and there is a serious conflict, ideological or otherwise, among coalition partners, some parliamentary decisions may reflect sectional electoral interests rather than the long-term interests of the people as a whole. There may also be times when the political or private interests of a leader of a ruling party or a group of leaders may be under public scrutiny because of certain exogenous or endogenous developments. In such exceptional, and one hopes infrequent, circumstances, it is necessary to have a court of last resort for deciding on the Constitutional validity of specific laws or actions initiated by the legislature or the executive. The final legal arbiter in such cases can only be the judiciary, which is directly accessible to the public, and whose verdicts are in any case subject to review and appeal.

It is, of course, true that the judiciary can also make mistakes. In view of the enormous delays and multiple levels of appeals, it can also be argued that the judicial system itself is in urgent need of reform in order to provide speedy justice. However, even after taking all these imperfections into account, I have no doubt that, on balance, the country is better off with the judiciary as an additional check point on the legality of actions taken (or, for the matter, not taken) by the legislature and the executive. It should be free to issue appropriate directions to any agency of the State if its actions are considered arbitrary, partisan, and violative of the intent of the Constitution in order to give India a government of the people, by the people, and for the people.

Let me end this chapter with two quotations from the eminent jurist, Nani Palkhivala, from his book, *We, the People*, published in 1984.[11] Commenting on the solemn declarations made by parliamentarians from time to time as being the supreme representatives of the will of the people, he had this to say:

> The myth that Parliament's will is the people's will was exploded at the election held in March 1977. Did the Parliament which [had earlier] passed the Forty-Second Amendment and which also approved of the proclamation of the emergency, represent the will of the people? . . . It is inconceivable that after having provided the most complete and comprehensive guarantees of the basic human freedoms known to any constitution of the world, the Constitution-makers still intended that any Parliament could take away those fundamental rights (p. 209 & p. 216).

And finally, on the sanctity of the Constitution, he reminded us and the generations yet to come:

> The Constitution is not a structure of fossils like a coral reef and is not intended merely to enable politicians to play their unending game of power. It is meant to hold the country together when the raucous and fractious voices of today are lost in the silence of the centuries (p. xv).

After nearly sixty years of independence, the vision of India's founding fathers of a rapidly growing, free, and empowered country is now closer to reality than ever before. The Constitution, which, as Nani Palkhivala rightly reminded us, is not 'a structure of fossils', must respond to the emerging realities of India's political life. Legislative norms and conventions must also ensure that politics serves the interests of the people rather than the other way round. This is the subject of the next chapter.

References

1. 'Question for Congress', Editorial, *Indian Express*, New Delhi, 19 April 2006, p. 8.

2. J.K. Ray (2001), *India: In Search of Good Governance*, Calcutta: K.K. Bagchi and Company. See also Chapter 3 on 'Crisis of Governance' in B. Jalan (2005), *The Future of India*, New Delhi: Viking-Penguin.

3. *Report of the National Commission to Review the Working of the Constitution* (2002), Government of India, New Delhi, p. 124.

4. D. Banik (1999), *The Transfer Raj: Indian Civil Servants on the Move*, Centre for Development and Environment, Oslo.

5. R. Gandhi (1989), cited in *India Today*, 30 November 1989, p. 16.

6. T.S.R. Subramaniam (2004), 'All the Netaji's Men', *Indian Express*, 25 September 2004, p. 9.

7. S. Shekhar and S. Balakrishnan (1999), *Voices from the Capital: A Report Card on Public Service in Delhi*, Public Affairs Centre, Bangalore.

8. T. Singh (2004), 'Fifth Column', *Indian Express*, 19 September 2004, p. 7.

9. This section is based on the Third Nani A. Palkhivala Memorial Lecture, *Separation of Powers: The Myth and the Reality*, delivered by the author on 16 January 2006 under the aegis of the Nani A. Palkhivala Memorial Trust, Mumbai.

10. S. Chatterjee (2005), *The Scheme of Separation of Powers and Checks and Balances in the Constitution*, Second Nani Palkhivala Memorial Lecture, Bar Association of India, 12 May 2005, New Delhi.

11. N.A. Palkhivala (1984), *We, the People*, Mumbai: Strand Book Store (new edition, 1994).

SIX

The Reform of Politics in a Resurgent India

The previous chapters have covered a wide range of issues on the emerging political scene in contemporary India, and their impact on different aspects of economic and social life. In this last chapter, I propose to look ahead and examine how the political system could be made to work better for the people as a whole rather than only for the few.

By its very nature, democracy, as they say, is a 'messy' business. All citizens are proud of it, but they are also impatient with the way it works. There is discontent with several of its features, such as the persistent antagonism among political parties and their leaders, delays in the decision-making process, conflicts among different organs of the State at the highest levels about their relative jurisdictions, and the prevalence of corruption and unethical practices among people in political life. India is not alone in this respect. In many of the older democracies (including the United States, UK, France, Italy and Germany), ordinary citizens have similar complaints about the working of their political systems. No one, except on the extremist fringe, would wish for any other form of government than a democracy that provides multiple freedoms. At the same time, all citizens want the system to work more efficiently in order to achieve higher growth and better distribution.

There is no shortage of ideas or suggestions on what should be done to improve governance and administration under a popularly elected government. In India, we have had multiple Administrative Reforms Commissions (one more such commission is currently at work—in the year 2007). We also have Finance Commissions, the Planning Commission (which is a standing body at the highest levels of the government), and other commissions to 'reform' the economy and establish a forward-looking regulatory framework for the agencies of the State. A high-level National Commission to Review the Working of the Constitution was also set up under the chairmanship of Justice Venkatachaliah in February 2000. The commission submitted its report in March 2002 and made a number of recommendations, some of which require amendments to the Constitution. The commission's recommendations cover a wide range of political, economic, social and legal issues, including Union–state relations and the working of Parliament and state legislatures. No action has so far been taken on any of the commission's recommendations, and according to available information, this report is no longer under active consideration by the government, or, for that matter, Parliament.

My purpose here is much more limited and modest

than those of the high-level commissions that are set up from time to time by the government. It is to suggest a few core changes (ten in number, to be precise) that respond to some of the emerging political and economic problems in the light of the analysis presented in previous chapters. The proposed limited agenda is designed to bridge the gap between economics and politics so that India can realize its full, and widely heralded, potential in the years ahead.

Before I come to the specific proposals, it may be useful to mention a couple of changes that have figured in the public debate but which, in my view, need *not* be pursued. The first is the proposal to convert India's parliamentary form of government into a presidential one. The second suggestion is to introduce a proportional system of elections to choose peoples' representatives in legislatures and Parliament in place of the prevailing 'first past the post' system. In theory, both these suggestions have much to commend themselves. They are also prevalent in several democracies around the world. However, in my view, it is neither necessary nor desirable to replace the existing system of voting and formation of government that has been in place since India became independent sixty years ago. Notwithstanding some of its shortcomings, the present system has proved to be resilient. Established conventions, judicial pronouncements, and legislative practice—based on consensus—are also vital in a multi-party federal republic like India.

It may also be mentioned that the alternatives to a parliamentary system have their own disadvantages.

They have worked well in some countries, but not in others. Thus, in the past, some countries with a presidential form of government in Africa and Latin America have found themselves in deep and persistent economic crises because of lack of checks and balances within the executive branch. When circumstances are favourable and the economy is doing well, a single and progressive centre of executive authority can be an advantage in accelerating growth and initiating policies that may not be politically popular. However, during periods when the economy is facing an unexpected challenge or crisis (for example, in the aftermath of the East Asian economic crisis of 1997), a single centre of executive authority may not be as effective. It is also likely that in a presidential form of government, the chief executive would be less sensitive to the need for a change in the policies initiated by him or her even if the actual results turn out to be negative.

Similarly, the system of proportional representation certainly has the advantage of reflecting the will of the people better than the system of simple majority verdicts. However, this alternative to a simple voting system is unduly complicated. It is also likely to be non-transparent for a large number of voters, more so when the levels of literacy and education among voters are very low. In practice, it may not reduce political instability if there are a large number of parties contesting the elections and if local issues, rather than national issues, dominate voter preferences.

On the whole, taking into account the experiences of other countries, I do not believe that any fundamental change is required in the form of government in India and the manner in which it is chosen. It is feasible to take measures, some of which may require amendments to the Constitution, to deal adequately with the emergent and pressing problems in India's politics. These are discussed below.

An Agenda for the Future

The proposed agenda for the future is necessarily selective and not comprehensive. I have no illusion that the necessary changes to make the present system more accountable and strengthen the democratic process would be easy to accept or implement because of the inherent conflicts of interest among different sections of the political spectrum. However, I believe that this is a minimum—and practical—agenda that deserves consideration and debate in legislative bodies, media and other institutions of the civil society.

(i) A Federation of States

Articles 245 to 255 of the Constitution of India deal with the distribution of powers between the Union and the states. The Centre has exclusive powers to make laws in respect of matters enumerated in the Union List (such as defence, foreign relations, and financial matters concerning the whole of India). The states have exclusive powers to make laws in respect of matters enumerated in the State List. These generally include matters where uniformity across the different states in respect of legal and administrative matters is not considered necessary (such as internal law and order, agriculture, and trade and commerce within a state). There is also the Concurrent List under which both the Union and the states can make laws. These include matters where the Centre can make laws applicable to all of India, but where individual states are also entitled to pass laws of specific interest to them. The residual powers, i.e. powers to make laws on any subject that is not listed in any of the above lists rest with the Union (unlike certain other federations, such as the United States, where the residual powers are with the states). The Centre also has the powers to make laws that are applicable to two or more states, if the concerned states so request, on a matter listed in the State List.

The above scheme for the distribution of powers between the Union and the states has stood the test of time, and is a tribute to the foresight of the framers of India's Constitution. In a country with such great diversity in languages, religions, castes, and levels of development, this scheme has proved to be a major unifying force among different states. All states are represented in the two Houses of the Union Parliament. In Parliament, they work together on the treasury benches or in the Opposition. Regional issues and matters of interest to particular states are open to discussion in Parliament, and are generally resolved through a consensus. There are, of course, long-standing interstate disputes (particularly on water or sources of energy), which flare up from time to time. However, even these have not threatened the unity of India because of the Union's conciliatory role and the representation of most states in the Union Cabinet.

In the economic and financial areas, over and above the Constitutional division of powers, an important development after Independence was the setting up of the Planning Commission and the launching of the First Five-Year Plan in 1951. Unlike the Finance Commission, which is an autonomous statutory body set up under the Constitution every five years to make recommendations on the formulae for the distribution of certain taxes among states, the Planning Commission was set up by a Resolution of the Government of India in March 1950. The chairperson of the Planning Commission is the prime minister; and there are five or six full-time members, who are appointed by the Central government. The Commission has been given the responsibility of preparing the five-year Plans for the country as a whole. Within the five-year Plan framework, it also approves the Annual Plans of the Centre as well as the state governments. For financing the plans and programmes approved by it every year, the Commission makes grants and loans to the states. Resources for this purpose are provided by the Central Budget.

As is well known, after more than a century of economic stagnation and low levels of industrialization during the colonial period, an important plank of the post-Independence development strategy was to make India economically independent through a faster pace of industrialization. The Planning Commission was set up as the primary instrument for achieving this goal through the acceleration of public investment by the Centre and the states in different areas of the economy, particularly industry and infrastructure.

Along with the setting up of the Planning Commission,
measures were taken to increase the scope and scale
of taxation by the Centre in order to provide additional
resources for financing the Plans. In the 1960s, the
Central government also acquired a virtual monopoly
over financial savings in the country through the
nationalization of banks and insurance companies. As
a result of these developments, in addition to the
exclusive power of the Centre to formulate macro-
economic policies, the Union government became all-
powerful in determining the shape of the economy as
well as the pace of development in the different states.
The states continue to be responsible for formulating
the state Plans and for their annual budgets, but they
have virtually no autonomous powers to raise private
or public financial resources to finance their Plans.

In the context of recent political developments at
the Centre, and the emergence of multi-party coalitions
of different types and durations as a regular feature of
governments, it is necessary to review the present
division of powers between the Union and the states.
Earlier in the book, I had referred to the urgent need
for transferring the powers for the maintenance of
internal security to the Centre from the states because
of external terrorist linkages and other factors. In the
economic area, it is desirable to consider a reverse
transfer, i.e. powers and responsibility for financing
development programmes should be transferred from
the Centre to the states. At present, the states formulate
their Plans, but the responsibility for the approval and
provision of sufficient resources for implementing
them rests with the Centre. In the context of coalition

politics, a five-year Plan for a particular period may be launched by one multi-party coalition government in a state, and approved by another combination of parties in power at the Centre. However, shortly thereafter, there may be a change in the government in the state and/or at the Centre. With every change in government at the Centre, there is a change in the composition of the Planning Commission. The same is true at the state level. There is also a re-alignment of the political relationship between the parties in power at the Centre and in different states with a change in government. Since governments are political bodies and their decisions are discretionary, it is likely that the actual flow of Central Plan assistance to different states from year to year will be increasingly determined by the timings of elections and the party composition of the coalition governments at the Centre and the party or parties in power in different states.

So far, by and large, India has been exceedingly fortunate in having persons of calibre, integrity, and patriotism in the top leadership positions irrespective of the nature of the coalitions to which they belong. However, it cannot be taken for granted that this situation will continue indefinitely in the future. While the country still has the good fortune of having highly distinguished leaders at the helm, immediate action needs to be taken on two fronts. First, more financial powers and increased responsibility for the implementation of development programmes should be entrusted to the states. This is not because all states are likely to be more scrupulous or consistent in the exercise of their powers, but because greater transparency and competition among the states would at least ensure that the better governed states have easier access to financial resources and the opportunity to implement their programmes. Just as the Finance Commission is Constitutionally empowered to decide on the division of tax resources between the Centre and the states, a similar federal commission should be statutorily set up to decide on the devolution of all other forms of Central assistance. The allocation of non-tax Central assistance should be related exclusively to the implementation of approved anti-poverty and development programmes in physical terms, that is, the greater the success of a state in implementing a programme in relation to its target in quantative terms, the higher should be the allocation of Central funds to that state.

Second, all appointments in autonomous institutions, regulatory bodies, public enterprises, banks, and financial, educational, and cultural institutions in the public sector should be entrusted to specialized bodies set up on the same lines as the Union Public Service Commission (UPSC). These appointment boards should follow transparent procedures for recommending appointments to the top positions. Their recommendations should be invariably accepted by the government (as is the case with UPSC recommendations for entry into the civil services and other appointments under its purview). Similar procedures, at an arm's length from the government, may be adopted for top appointments in the civil services. Recent developments, and the controversies surrounding them, in many of India's top institutions, including centres of excellence in medicine and management, highlight the need for urgent action to insulate public institutions from excessive political interference in their day-to-day work.

(ii) The Council of States

As discussed in the earlier chapters, in respect of elections to the Council of States (i.e. the Rajya Sabha), the Representation of the People's Act, 1951 was amended by Parliament in August 2003. The two significant amendments were: (i) persons elected as members of the Rajya Sabha do not have to be residents of the states that elect them, and (ii) the secret voting procedure, which is applicable in all other elections, has been replaced by open voting. A dissenting member who votes against a party candidate is likely to be removed from his or her party as well as from the state legislature for indiscipline and defection.

At first glance, the above two amendments appear quite reasonable. It is a well-known fact that in the past some members who were not ordinarily residents of a state, had declared themselves to be residents of that state in order to qualify for elections to the Rajya Sabha. Similarly, it has also been noticed that some electors in state legislatures had voted in favour of candidates belonging to other parties in exchange for financial and other favours.

In practice, however, the combined effect of the above two amendments will have a substantial impact on the composition of the Rajya Sabha, and make the so-called Upper House of Parliament even less representative of the people than is the case at present. Neither the people of a state directly, nor their representatives in the state legislature indirectly, will have any voice or discretion in electing their representatives to the Rajya Sabha. The choice of members will now depend entirely and exclusively on the leaders of the various parties. Anyone with sufficient resources, organized manpower, and access to leaders can be elected from anywhere depending on the ability of a party to swing a sufficient number of votes in the state legislature. A system of *quid pro quo* among the parties is bound to develop where one party provides balancing support to another party in one state in exchange for similar support by that party in another state.

It is inevitable that, over a period of time, the composition of the Rajya Sabha will change in favour of persons who are financially well-off, persons who have a criminal background, and persons who need preferential access to the corridors of power. The Rajya Sabha is also likely to become a safe haven for leaders who fail to get elected to the Lok Sabha. Public-spirited individuals and those with a background of service to the people of a particular state will still get elected as nominees of different parties but, over a period of time, such cases are likely to become fewer in number. Taking into account the working of our system of parliamentary democracy with more than fifty parties being represented in the state legislatures and in Parliament, there is no doubt that over the next ten to fifteen years, the composition of the Rajya Sabha will have become vastly different from what was envisaged in the original Constitution.

In view of their negative implications, two former members of Parliament with highly distinguished records in the field of journalism (namely Kuldip Nayar and Inderjeet) filed a petition before the Supreme Court of India, challenging the validity of the above amendments. On 22 August 2006, a five-member Constitutional Bench gave its verdict. It opined that the above amendments were not un-Constitutional and did not violate the basic structure of the Constitution.

On the question of domicile, the main point made in the verdict of the Supreme Court was that there was no requirement in law that the person elected must possess the same qualifications as those possessed by the elector. It was, therefore, not necessary that a representative of a state elected by the legislative assembly of that state, must also be ordinary residents of the state. The Bench also disagreed with the view that the elections to the Rajya Sabha by legislators must necessarily be held by open voting. Here the point made by the Court was that the mode of voting depended on whether elections were direct or indirect. While secret voting was essential for direct elections, it was not so in respect of indirect elections.

The above verdict was given by a five-member Constitutional Bench of the highest court in the land. It has to be accepted as being fully justified in so far as the legal issues are concerned. However, as mentioned above, the issues involved also have important long-term political ramifications, which are necessarily outside the jurisdiction of the courts. The political issue is simply whether the Rajya Sabha members elected under the present procedures are at all politically qualified to represent the interests of their states in a manner that is different from or more competent than representation by directly elected members from the same states in the Lok Sabha. This is the larger political issue. It is similar to the question considered by the Constituent Assembly on whether India should be a federation or a union of states without separate legislative assemblies. Legally, for the framers of the Indian Constitution, both the options were open. They finally decided to go for one of the above options in view of the larger social and political issues involved.

On larger political grounds rather than on legal grounds, the above two amendments dealing with elections to the Rajya Sabha deserve to be rescinded as early as possible by Parliament itself. There can hardly be any doubt that, even with some shortcomings, the earlier system represented the interests of the states better than the present one. Alternatively, if it is considered necessary to reduce the discretion available to the people's representatives in the state legislatures, then direct elections by the people may be considered. Direct elections to both the Houses of a legislature are already prevalent in many democracies, including the United States.

A reform of the present system for elections to the Rajya Sabha is urgent. If it is not politically feasible to reform the electoral process, it would be much better for the functioning of India's democracy to have a unicameral Parliament, as is already the case in some states of India. This will not only save time and budgetary resources but will also prevent further erosion in the federal character of the Indian Union.

One argument against having a unicameral legislature is that it may affect the quality of the Cabinet. This may happen in case some prominent and qualified persons belonging to a political party (which is called upon to form the government) happen to lose the Lok Sabha elections or are not inclined to contest elections. At present, they can be elected to the Rajya Sabha and are able to find places in the Cabinet if their party so desires. The same is true of some highly qualified persons from different professions, industry, and trade. These concerns are valid. It is in the larger public interest for the prime minister to be able to appoint the most qualified persons in the country to the Cabinet. However, this objective can be achieved by adopting a Constitutional amendment to the effect that a government with a majority in Parliament can, if it so wishes, appoint, say, up to 25 per cent of members of the Cabinet from outside Parliament. Those who are appointed in this manner, may be authorized to participate fully in the proceedings of the Lok Sabha in their ministerial capacity without having the right to vote. Interestingly, this is precisely the case now in respect of members of the Rajya Sabha who are appointed to the Cabinet. They are able to participate fully in the proceedings of the Lok Sabha without a right to vote in that House.

(iii) State Funding of Elections

This issue has been considered from time to time in Parliament and other fora. However, so far no consensus has emerged even though there is general agreement that the need to collect large funds for elections is a primary cause of political corruption. It is also a known fact that, over time, while large amounts are being raised in the name of political parties, a substantial portion of such funds are being diverted for personal use. The print and electronic media have exposed several high-profile cases of the accumulation of illicit wealth by chief ministers, ministers, and other leaders in and out of office.

It is obvious that, given the large number of persons with criminal records who are active in politics, state funding of elections will not eliminate corruption entirely. However, it would at least help those who want to remain in politics without having to indulge in corruption. State funding may also help in reducing the acceptability by the general public of corruption as an unavoidable fact of Indian political life and strengthen the hands of some public-spirited non-governmental organizations (NGOs) in their fight against corruption.

One argument that is frequently advanced against state funding is that it would favour large parties and would, therefore, be unfair to small or new parties. Another argument is that the fiscal cost of such funding will be high and unbearable for many states as well as the Centre. While there is indeed some merit in both arguments, these are by no means persuasive and compelling.

To take the second argument first, the size of the Budget expenditure by the Central government for the year 2005–06 is estimated to be of the order of Rs

550,000 crore. One percent of this amount would yield as much as Rs 5,500 crore for financing Lok Sabha elections and for providing some support to the state governments for holding state elections. Even if such elections are held twice every five years (because of greater political instability), the amount of Rs 5,500 crore is sufficient to provide Rs 5 crore to Rs 10 crore for each Lok Sabha constituency. In terms of the Central Budget, the amount to be earmarked for elections would thus vary from 0.2 to 0.4 per cent of the total expenditure annually (depending on the frequency of elections). By no means can this be regarded as an unbearable fiscal burden for a cause as vital as election funding.

The size of the total budgetary expenditure by the state governments is twice as large as that of the Central government, i.e. about Rs 1,100,000 crore in 2005–06. One per cent of this amount is Rs 11,000 crore. This should be more than sufficient to provide adequate support to recognized political parties for fighting state elections once or twice in a five-year cycle.

It may also be mentioned that the Central government allocates nearly Rs 1,700 crore annually to fund the Members of Parliament Local Area Development (MPLAD) scheme. State governments have similar schemes for their Members of Legislative Assemblies (MLAs). In view of the significant misuse of such allocations, as highlighted by the electronic and print media in 2006 (which led to the expulsion of several MPs), it is desirable to discontinue MPLAD-type schemes both at the Centre and in the states.

From the country's point of view, it would be much better if budgetary funds allocated for such schemes were used for election funding.

In the book *The Future of India*, I had suggested a possible scheme for the equitable distribution of electoral funds among large and small political parties.[1] The proposed distribution formula is by no means perfect, but it should broadly meet the legitimate concerns of small parties. Let me briefly recapitulate the main features of a workable and practical scheme of distribution:

- Funds for elections to recognized political parties should be provided under two broad heads: (a) to reimburse certain categories of identified election expenditure; and (b) to meet a relatively small amount of residual expenditure on staff and for the maintenance of party election offices.

- A predetermined category of actual expenditure, which should be eligible for reimbursement, could cover newspaper and television advertising for a specified period, say, two or three weeks prior to elections and reasonable transport costs by air and train for election campaigns. Rules for the reimbursement of actual expenses under these (and any other admissible heads) may be laid down by the Election Commission. Advertising by political parties may be limited to the amount that is eligible for re-imbursement. In other words, parties that benefit from state funding for advertising should not be allowed to spend any additional amount under this head on their own account. They can incur additional expenditure on their own, if they wish, on all other items, such as staff and offices.

- The division between 'large' and 'small' parties for the purposes of allocation of funds may be made according to a benchmark, approved by Parliament after appropriate consultations with the Election Commission. Thus, parties with, say, a minimum of 10 or 15 per cent of seats in the Lok Sabha or the state legislatures (for state elections) may be considered to be 'large' parties. All other parties may be considered to be small parties.

- Reimbursement of actual expenditure under the prescribed heads may be the same for all 'large' parties (as defined by Parliament for this purpose) and proportionately less for smaller parties (depending on the actual number of seats held by them in the Lok Sabha or the state legislatures).

- Allocation of funds to meet residual expenditure on staff and offices may be weighted by the number of seats held by each party. The weights may be suitably devised to ensure that the larger the party, the higher is its entitlement to funds on this account, but that small parties are not put to an undue disadvantage.

As a large and vibrant democracy, India is not alone in facing the problems of electoral funding through legitimate means. As the *Economist*, London observed in respect of Britain, 'If Britain's two biggest political parties were companies, they would be in trouble for trading while insolvent!'[2] The costs of contesting elections in India and elsewhere have increased phenomenally in recent years because of changes in the methods of communication. In addition to personal campaigning, the use of the electronic media for sending messages to voters has become unavoidable in all democracies. While costs have increased, and there are several elections to fight every year at different levels (i.e. national, state and district), contributions from reliable sources have dwindled. Fewer persons now become party members or make contributions to political parties. The same is true of charitable organizations and the corporate sector.

In order to partly overcome these problems, some of the old as well as the new democracies, including Britain and the United States, have introduced some funding of political parties through transparent and verifiable rules. India must do the same as early as feasible.

(iv) The Role of Small Parties in Government

In a democratic State, every citizen has a legitimate right to vote, contest elections and launch a political party. If a political party enjoys the minimum electoral support prescribed by the Election Commission, it is recognized as a national or regional party. At the national level, regional parties are also eligible to join a coalition government. Irrespective of the size of their representation in Parliament, they can continue to function as separate parliamentary parties with their own agenda. In principle, this is a reasonable arrangement in a multi-party and diverse country with a federal Constitution like that of India.

An important principle of parliamentary democracy is that the government is formed with the support of a majority of directly elected members in the House of the People (i.e. the Lok Sabha in India). Each member has a single and equal vote. Once a government is formed, whether by one party or by a number of parties in a coalition, it is supposed to be collectively responsible to Parliament and, through it, to the people.

Unfortunately, these fundamental principles of parliamentary democracy have been compromised in India in recent years. As we have seen in earlier chapters, small parties, with less than 5 per cent of the national votes and an even smaller number of members in Parliament, now command a disproportionate influence as partners in a coalition government. Even a collective decision of the Cabinet can be shelved or overturned at the insistence of a supporting regional party. If the coalition government consists of a number of small parties, and is also dependent for survival on the support of other parties outside the coalition, then the situation becomes even more complicated. The government may continue in office, but it is unlikely to enjoy sufficient political authority for ensuring efficient governance.

Another consequence of the formation of governments with the inside and outside support of a large number of small parties has been political instability, or at least the threat of it. After 1989, as many as six governments were not able to complete their full-term. This was also the case in respect of two coalition governments that were briefly in office during the period 1977–79 (after the Emergency of 1975 was lifted). It is also worth recalling that two of the worst economic crises faced by India, in 1979 and 1990, were in no small measure due to the inability of the governments then in power to take timely corrective action because of uncertainty and periodic threats to their survival in office.

From time to time, political uncertainty and instability are unavoidable in a parliamentary democracy with a large number of parties with conflicting interests. However, if this becomes a regular feature over a long stretch of time, it is important to ensure that all parties that form a coalition function collectively in order to provide efficient public administration. To this end, it is particularly desirable to reduce the disproportionate power enjoyed by small parties that decide to join a coalition.

At present, a small party is free to join a coalition and hold crucial ministerial berths. At the same time, if it so decides, it is also free to follow its own regional or sectoral agenda in the exercise of its ministerial responsibility. In case it is dissatisfied with a decision of the Cabinet, it can threaten to walk out of the coalition and reduce the government to a minority. In order to avoid fresh elections, it can continue to support the government from outside if and when a no-confidence motion is moved by the Opposition. In this way, the members of a defecting party can continue in Parliament/legislatures. At the appropriate time, they can also join another coalition.

As mentioned earlier, in order to prevent defections by individuals or groups of members of a party in Parliament/legislature, in 1985 and again in 2003, the Constitution was amended to disqualify them from continuing as members or from holding any other public office until their re-election. A similar measure should be introduced to disqualify members of a party (with say, less than 10 or 15 per cent of seats in the Lok Sabha, as may be decided by Parliament), who opt to join a coalition and then decide to defect. It should be made mandatory for all members of such a party to seek re-election. As provided in the 2003 amendment, members of a defecting party should also not be permitted to hold any public or ministerial offices during the remaining part of the term of Parliament/legislatures. There is no justifiable reason why members of a small party should be put in a more favourable position than any other group of defecting members. Indeed, it can be argued that the present system provides a built-in incentive for the fragmentation of a large party into smaller separate parties at the time of elections. The leader of a small party enjoys all the benefits of being part of a larger party formation (e.g. occupying a ministerial berth) without any of its disadvantages.

The above rules should also apply to 'independent' members who opt to join a coalition government. Further, in order to reduce the threat of political instability, it is also desirable to introduce an amendment to the rules of business in Parliament. It may be provided that all parties in the government should become members of the same parliamentary party under the banner of their coalition. They should not be recognized as separate parties for purposes of parliamentary business. Thus, for example, the NDA or the UPA or any other coalition that forms the government should be considered as the NDA or the UPA parliamentary party as long as it is in office. Such an amendment will have the salutary effect of formally recognizing all parties in a coalition as a joint parliamentary party for conducting the business of government in Parliament/legislatures. All such parties may, of course, continue to have their separate identity for all other purposes, including the power to nominate their own candidates during elections.

(v) The Business of Parliament

In an earlier chapter, we had reviewed the proceedings in Parliament towards the end of March 2006 during the Budget session. Even after taking into account the observed decline in recent years in the role of Parliament in shaping the nation's policy priorities, the events of March 2006 were nothing short of bizarre. The Budget and the Finance Bill were passed without sufficient notice within a couple of days. The government also suddenly decided to adjourn Parliament *sine die* in the middle of the session only to reconvene it again after a few days. During the resumed session, the controversy about Members of Parliament (including high-ranking dignitaries) holding so-called offices of profit reached its culmination. As per the existing rules, members are not eligible to hold 'offices of profit' unless specifically exempted by

Parliament. In May 2006, the government proposed, and the Parliament disposed, a new Bill to exempt some specific offices at the Centre and the states, depending on whether these offices were held by sitting Members of Parliament. Thus, the same office (say, the chairmanship of the Waqf Board) was exempted in one state because a current member was holding this office, but not in other states of the Union. The details of this controversy are not important for our purpose here; what is important is to recognize that in India's long parliamentary legislative history, the passage of this Bill marked a new low.

If proof were needed for corroborating the above conclusion, this was amply provided by the refusal of the President of India to give assent to the Bill as passed by Parliament. For the first time after the adoption of India's Constitution, the President sent the Bill back to Parliament, along with his observations, for reconsideration. The government, in its wisdom, decided to place the same Bill for approval by Parliament without responding to the Constitutional issues raised by the President. Despite the reservations of several members, Parliament duly approved the bill once again, as proposed by the government.

This extraordinary and unprecedented event was followed by several unsavoury controversies in July–August 2006 involving certain decisions taken by the Cabinet, a book by the Leader of the Opposition in the Rajya Sabha, and allegations of wrongdoing by a former minister of external affairs. Charges and counter-charges were hurled across the floor of the two Houses from all sides. In view of the noisy disruptions, Parliament had to be adjourned several times. The Speaker and the Chairman of the two Houses tried to control and direct the proceedings, but to no avail. The well-established rules of procedure for the conduct of business in the Houses of Parliament were also largely ignored. Any citizen watching the proceedings of Parliament from inside or outside (on dedicated TV channels) could not but be dismayed by the persistent chaos and lawlessness in the highest legislative body of the largest democracy in the world.

It is also significant that, in the midst of all this noise and disruption, the so-called government business was duly carried out, including the adoption of several legislative Bills. Since the government Bills, resolutions, and statements could not be discussed because of frequent disruptions, these were adopted by voice votes within a couple of minutes (with very few members even being aware of the fact that they were actually voting!). As a result, the passage of important government Bills in Parliament has now become a mere formality.

It does not really matter whether Parliament meets or not; what the government wants to do is done in one way or another. The notion of the responsibility of the executive to the legislature is also largely a myth, and of no particular consequence. There are, of course, occasions when debates in Parliament on important national issues (such as the nuclear agreement between India and the United States) are of exceptionally high quality and when the government is responsive to the concerns expressed by members in Parliament. However, even such vital international

agreements and treaties can be signed by the
government without the need for approval or
ratification by Parliament.

In the era of coalition governments, the
responsibility of Parliament for enforcing the
accountability of the multi-party executive has
increased but, unfortunately, its power to do so has
diminished. In order to restore the relevance of
Parliament in a parliamentary democracy, it is now
imperative to take measures to make its proceedings
orderly. There must be strict rules of business, which
should not be altered or violated with impunity. A
possible approach for achieving this objective could
be as follows:

- In theory, the Speaker and the Chairman have
  the powers to expel a member from the House
  or to suspend him or her. But these powers
  have seldom been exercised. A convention has
  also developed whereby the House can be
  adjourned several times during the day for a
  whole week or more in the event of disruption
  by a few members. It may be specifically
  provided, by legislation, that either House of
  Parliament cannot be adjourned more than
  twice in a week unless the listed business,
  including the carried over business from
  previous sessions, has been completed after
  full discussion as per the time allotted by the
  Business Advisory Committees of Parliament.
- No Bill or legislative business of the government
  should be approved by a 'voice vote'. It should
  be made compulsory to adopt all Bills after

division and counting of votes. This would require one or two hours of additional time to pass a Bill, which is not excessive. If, because of unruly behaviour and disruption by members, a Bill cannot be discussed and voted upon, then so be it. In case the matter is considered urgent or if there is a national emergency, the Speaker/Chairman should be empowered to convene a special session, during which no other matter can be raised.

- A legislative provision may be made to the effect that the established rules of procedure for the conduct of business of the House cannot be suspended or amended after a session of Parliament has been formally convened, except in a national emergency declared by the government with the approval of the President. In other words, ad hoc and sudden suspension of the rules of business, as was done in March 2006, should not be permitted.

- It should be made compulsory for the Budget and the Finance Bill to be passed only after consideration by the concerned standing committees of Parliament. This rule, which is already in place, should be made compulsory. If for any reason (such as election schedules), sufficient time is not available, then only a 'vote-on-account' should be passed by Parliament.

- The Speaker/Chairman should be required mandatorily to suspend or expel members who frequently disrupt the House. If members from any side of the House (those belonging to the ruling parties or to the parties in the Opposition) disrupt the work of the House on, say, more than two occasions in a week, it should be incumbent on the Speaker/Chairman to continue with the session (by suspending or expelling the defaulting members) rather than adjourn the House.

The above rules will by no means eliminate all the problems that affect the functioning of Parliament, but will certainly help in making its sessions more purposeful.

(vi) *The Reform of Government*

In India, governments at the Centre and the states, along with their agencies, have practically unlimited powers to pass laws, notify rules and regulations and determine economic and social priorities. Some of these may require parliamentary or legislative approval but as we have noted above, as long as a government has the requisite majority, such approval is a formality. While the available powers are enormous, it is also a fact that the authority of the government to actually enforce laws and rules is minimal. Part of the reason is, of course, judicial delays. However, as recognized by the government at the highest levels, one-third to one-fourth of Indian districts are now under Naxalite influence, where the laws of the state or the Centre are largely inoperative.

Several surveys and opinion polls have also provided telling statistics about the extent of corruption in government agencies. Some years ago one such survey by the Public Affairs Centre, based in Bangalore, found that every fourth person in one of the large cities in India ends up paying a bribe when dealing with agencies such as those for urban development, electricity, municipal services, and telephones.[3] This was the position some years ago. Since then, the position has become much worse, and every other person needs to pay a bribe or engage a 'tout' to get these or any other licence or service.

Interestingly, despite the deepening crisis of governance, as discussed earlier, India is currently witnessing a new growth momentum. This paradox is largely explained by three factors. First, beginning in the early 1980s, the heavy hand of the government in controlling the role of non-governmental sectors in manufacturing as well as services was lifted. A second factor was the gradual opening up of the economy through reduction in protective tariffs and the abolition of import and export quotas of various types. India became an attractive global destination for capital, skills, and business outsourcing. Finally, particularly after the Asian crisis in 1997, India managed its external sector exceedingly well. After nearly four decades of periodic crises (beginning in 1956), India emerged as a country with a strong balance of payments and with one of the highest levels of foreign exchange reserves. It is interesting to note that all the three factors were related to positive changes in macro-economic policies, which created a more competitive environment, and removed extensive governmental controls over individual and corporate initiatives. These had very little to do with institutional or micro-level changes in the administrative and governance structures within the government.

The fact that the overall rate of growth has accelerated due to a resurgence in the private sector of the economy makes the need for reforms within the government even more urgent, not less. In a poor country with a large population where the bulk of the people are dependent on agriculture and have access to few basic amenities, a high rate of growth in national income by itself cannot reduce disparities or remove poverty. Government intermediation in favour of a more equitable distribution of the benefits of growth through the provision of public services and public investment in basic infrastructure is essential. Even if we assume that as many as 200 or 250 million people are currently benefiting from the high rates of growth in manufacturing and services in the private sector, more than 800 million persons in India would still continue to be at the periphery of the circles of prosperity for quite some time. Meanwhile, the widening of disparities among different sections of the people can cause severe strains in the political and social life of the country.

The kind of reforms that are required and feasible in the current political scenario is a matter on which there is likely to be vast differences of opinion among experts and others. The subject has been discussed at great length in reports issued by the Planning Commission in the context of the formulation of the Eleventh Five-Year Plan (2008–13) as well as other specialized committees set up by the government. Let

me mention only a few vital principles that, in my
view, need to be adopted as early as possible in order
to guide the process of reforms in the next few years:

- The political role of the government in the
  economy needs to be redefined and prioritized.
  At the macro-economic level, the political (i.e.
  ministerial) role of the government should be
  to ensure a stable and competitive environment
  with a strong external sector and a transparent
  domestic financial system. While the macro-
  economic priorities (for example, the trade-off
  between growth and inflation) may be decided
  by the government, the instrumentalities for
  achieving these objectives must be left to
  autonomous regulatory and promotional
  agencies.
- The government's direct role in economic areas
  must be re-set in favour of ensuring the
  availability of public goods (such as roads and
  water) and essential services (such as health
  and education) to the people. In these areas,
  the government's role must expand
  substantially. At the same time, its role in
  managing commercial enterprises deserves to
  be correspondingly reduced. The latter objective
  should be achieved without in any way affecting
  the financial and other benefits of those who
  are presently employed.
- Another important priority is the simplification
  of administrative procedures and the reduction
  in the number of agencies, at different levels,
  involved in providing clearances for

undertaking any activity. This is an area where the supply of corruption by public servants creates its own demand. Thus, for example, at least thirty different clearances, involving several agencies at the Centre and the states, are required for setting up even a modest-sized industrial factory. Except in selected areas involving paramount national interests (such as security and defence), it is desirable to cut through the elaborate red tape and rely primarily on 'self-certification'. The government can lay down standards and norms (for example, in respect of environmental impact or safety), and the entity concerned may be required to 'self-certify' that these have been complied with as per the notified procedures. Government agencies can make random checks and in case there are violations, appropriate penal action can be taken. Similarly, the present complexity in regulations should be reduced drastically. Such simplification has been tried out in some areas with success (for example, in foreign exchange transactions).

• A related area is transparency in the decision-making process within the government. A major step in this respect has been taken with the enactment of the Right to Information Act, 2005. The beneficial impact of this legislation in making the government accountable and citizen-friendly is already visible. A further step in this direction is to make it mandatory for all ministries and departments of the government to voluntarily make information on the decisions taken by them available to the public (excluding security-related subjects). It may be clarified that information should be released by the ministries themselves without the need for any member of the public to ask for it. If this is done, the free media and civil society institutions will constitute an effective instrument for enforcing accountability in the decision-making process itself.

• Case studies of international experience in the management of public services show that the objective of such programmes can be achieved better, and at less cost, if a distinction is made between the ownership of these services (by the government) and the delivery of such services (by non-governmental organizations and local enterprises).[4] In such cases, the public authorities retain the responsibility for regulating and monitoring the activities, providing subsidies where necessary, and laying down distribution guidelines. In India, two noteworthy examples of public–private collaboration in the area of public services are: the public call offices (PCOs), which revolutionalized the availability of telephone services all over the country in the 1990s, and the Sulabh Sauchalayas, which, despite some problems, are estimated to have provided sanitation facilities to around ten million people at very low cost.

The above suggestions are by no means exhaustive. However, I believe that these, along with some other suggestions given below, should help immensely in making the government 'of the people and by the people' work effectively for the benefit of the people.

(vii) Ministerial Responsibility

A minister as the political head of a ministry enjoys enormous executive powers. Part of the rationale for entrusting politically appointed ministers, of whom several have very little previous administrative experience, is that the ministry is supposed to be accountable to the Cabinet and to Parliament though them.

While the above system is sound in principle, in practice there has been a substantial erosion in the ability of Parliament/legislatures to hold ministers responsible, either collectively or individually, for the decisions taken by them on behalf of their ministries. In addition to the principle of collective responsibility (which shields ministers from taking individual responsibility), another reason why ministers are not held accountable is that most subjects of direct interest to the public in the economic area are in the Concurrent or State Lists of business. The Central ministers are free to make pronouncements, approve policy guidelines and set all-India targets, but the actual implementation of programmes happens to be in the hands of individual states. A familiar excuse given by Central ministers for their failure in meeting the targets announced by them is that the states are responsible and not the Centre. The states, on the other hand, blame the Centre for inadequate allocation of funds, inappropriate guidelines or approval delays by one or more ministries at the Centre. The present situation, where the Central ministers are quick to announce policies and targets for removing poverty or illiteracy but where they take no responsibility for achieving these targets, is clearly untenable.

Assuming that political parties, civil society, and the enlightened members of the Indian public are serious about removing the worst forms of poverty and deprivation, then a new institutional initiative is urgently required for enforcing ministerial responsibility for the efficient delivery of public services and anti-poverty programmes all over the country. This can be achieved only if the cherished doctrine of collective and concurrent responsibility for all actions of the government is replaced by the notion of individual responsibility of ministers for implementing the programmes that they announce. The doctrine of collective responsibility can continue to prevail for all other political purposes, including the continuation of a government in office.

In future, the Planning Commission (or, Federal Commission; see above) should be made responsible for placing before Parliament a report on the actual achievements in relation to the agreed annual targets. This report should be the focal point of discussion in Parliament on a ministry's budget, and if there is a shortfall of more than the agreed percentage (say, 15 or 20 per cent), then the minister must be held responsible and should be expected to relinquish ministerial office for at least one year. Once an annual target is announced by a ministry, it should have the full authority to implement it, and it should be the only ministry that is held accountable for actual performance. If there is a change of ministers during the course of the year, then the new minister must once again affirm or change the target with the approval of Parliament.

Another area where immediate action is necessary is that of lowering the bar on political corruption. On the grounds of compulsions of coalition politics, the tolerance for political corruption at high levels of the government and Parliament/legislatures has increased significantly in recent years. A lid has to be put on the tolerance levels of corruption, at least at the ministerial level. Persons who have been 'charge-sheeted' for corruption, fraud, and similar criminal offences should not be permitted to take the oath of office and function as ministers until they are cleared by the courts. A special procedure may be set up to immediately hold and expedite court hearings in cases of persons who are proposed to be appointed as ministers.

(viii) Depoliticization of the Civil Services

A great deal has been written on the atrophy, non-accountability, corruption and ineptitude of the Indian civil services (Ray 2001).[5] In addition to academics and international agencies, this view has been expressed by a number of civil servants who have recounted their experiences after their retirement from the highest offices of the State. There is now almost complete unanimity that, despite having some of the best and the brightest persons in the civil services, the system as a whole has become non-functional.

As citizens, whether we like it or not, we need an efficient civil service, not only to provide basic services, but also to be able to carry on with the ordinary business of life. Unfortunately, the crisis in the civil services is now so deep and wide that the general view among experts and experienced civil servants seems to be that the reform of the system is not feasible. This is not because the country does not know what to do but because of political resistance to the reform of the civil service. Politicians at present enjoy substantial powers to coerce civil servants to do their bidding. In recent years, with the emergence of coalition politics as the norm at the Centre and in several states, and frequent changes in the composition of the Cabinet, the position has become worse.

The basic issue that needs to be tackled for improving the morale of the civil service is really that of the 'separation of powers' within the executive— between ministers and civil servants—insofar as postings, transfers, promotions, and other similar administrative matters are concerned. The separation of powers among the three branches of the government—the executive, the legislature, and the judiciary—is already enshrined in the Constitution. Although there has been considerable encroachment of the executive powers into the legislative, and even the judicial areas (and also the other way round), it can still be said that these three separate branches enjoy a certain measure of autonomy and independence. Within the executive branch, however, the civil service is now completely dependent on the pleasure of the ministers in regard to even the most mundane and routine administrative matters. It is essential to revert to a rule-based system of administration, which circumscribes the powers of politicians and confers greater authority on the civil service itself for self-regulation.

Similarly, while economic policy decisions can be taken by the Cabinet or its ministers, specific cases should invariably be decided by permanent administrative committees. They will, of course, be accountable to political authorities and, through them, to Parliament for the decisions taken by them.

The greater empowerment of the civil service must go hand in hand with the greater accountability of civil servants for their performance and ethical conduct. While, within the executive branch, the civil service has lost power, so far as the public is concerned, it is still the most powerful agency of the State. Part of the reason for the insensitivity of civil servants to the concerns of the public is the unlimited protection provided to the so-called 'public servants' under the Constitution and subsequent judicial pronouncements. In view of the time-consuming process of enquiries and judicial delays, the possibility of any penal action being taken for even the most blatant actions of civil servants is considered remote. They may be apprehended and sent to judicial custody for a few days. Thereafter, more often than not, they are released on bail and enjoy complete freedom of action, including the right to contest elections after retirement from the service.

Except for the security, police, and defence services, the Constitutional protection provided to civil servants needs to be withdrawn. They should be covered under the country's normal rules and laws, which are applicable to other citizens, employees, and workers. Two statutory provisions in particular, namely Article 311 of the Constitution and the Official Secrets Act, 1923 require urgent re-consideration. Article 311 provides comprehensive Constitutional protection, which has been widely misused, for a person holding a 'civil post from being reduced in rank, removed or dismissed from service'. The Official Secrets Act, 1923 provides protection to civil servants and ministers from being held accountable for any action that can be labelled as secret by them. The recent Right to Information Act, 2005 has substantially reduced the power of civil servants to deny information to the public. There is no reason why the 1923 Act should still remain valid.

It may be clarified that the withdrawal of Constitutional and special statutory protection provided to civil servants will not in any way affect their service conditions, pay, and other benefits. These will continue to be determined as per the present rules and procedures.

(ix) Fiscal Empowerment

The adoption of the Fiscal Responsibility and Budget Management Act (FRBM) in 2003 marked an important step towards fiscal consolidation. The FRBM Act mandates the gradual elimination of the 'revenue deficit' by 2009, and restricts the 'fiscal deficit' (i.e. market borrowings by the government) to a maximum of 3 per cent of GDP thereafter. Several state governments have also adopted similar legislation to eliminate or reduce their revenue and fiscal deficits over a period of time. The decision to reduce deficits means that, over the specified period, the government will have to reduce its borrowings from the market to finance various kinds of subsidies (on food or oil products, for example) as well as capital investment. In case subsidies and other politically mandated expenditure cannot be reduced, then capital expenditure as a percentage of GDP would necessarily have to decline in order to meet the FRBM target.

In view of the likely negative impact of the FRBM Act on public investment and socially desirable subsidies, there has been considerable debate on whether India should adopt a legislatively mandated fiscal target at all. In case such a target needs to be pursued, issues have also been raised about what precisely should be covered by such targets. Would it not be more appropriate to exclude interest payments on past borrowings or capital investments from the ambit of such targets? The Planning Commission is among the high-level government agencies that has questioned the appropriateness of fixing annual fiscal targets under the FRBM Act.

The above issues are no doubt relevant and appropriate. However, they do not resolve the fundamental issues relating to budgets and expenditure patterns that require the government's urgent attention. In India's current situation, with high foreign exchange reserves and relatively moderate rates of inflation, it is not all that vital whether the fiscal and revenue deficits are somewhat higher or lower than the targets specified in the FRBM Act. The only point that must be recognized is that there has to be some kind of a limit on government borrowings from the market or the Reserve Bank of India (in cash). Elementary common sense would suggest that if there were no need for such a 'cap', no developing country would have remained poor. It could simply grow to high levels of prosperity by means of unlimited borrowings and printing of its own currency.

The fundamental issue that requires attention relates to the present pattern of government expenditures, and the use to which resources raised through revenue or fiscal deficits are being put. If the deficit were used productively and could generate a sufficient rate of return to cover the repayment of past debt, the precise level of the deficit would not have mattered all that much. Alternatively, if the government's tax and non-tax revenues were in surplus over current expenditure (including subsidies), that surplus could be used to service past debt. Depending on the level of tolerance for inflationary pressures, and the growth rate of domestic savings, a certain amount of revenue or fiscal deficit could also be accepted without giving rise to financial instability and undue pressures on the economy.

In India, the basic problem is that the bulk of government expenditure is now devoted to the payment of salaries and the servicing of past debts. New programmes are launched but the governments are fiscally 'disempowered' from carrying them out. Despite large deficits, sufficient resources are not available for financing essential capital expenditure, improving public services, and undertaking even the routine maintenance of infrastructure. Fiscal disempowerment is not confined to rural areas; even the fastest growing cities are affected by the government's inability to provide civic amenities. For example, in the capital city of New Delhi, the *Delhi Human Development Report 2006*, released by the government, shows that the number of households without piped water and sanitation facilities actually increased during the decade of 1991–2001. This was the case despite the fact that Delhi is showing the fastest rate of growth in per capita incomes, which was two and a half times that of the national average and far higher than that of any other state in India. The government of Delhi and its agencies were still not in a position to find enough fiscal resources for providing basic services to the less better-off sections of the society or for improving the city's infrastructure.

The same is true of most other states of India. According to official statistics, despite sharp increases in resource transfers from the Centre and high revenue deficits, the total development expenditure of the state governments has actually been declining.[6] In 2005–06, total development expenditure (revenue plus capital) is estimated to be 9.4 per cent of GDP compared to 10.2 per cent in 2004–05. It is even more striking that, within the total development expenditure on all accounts, social sector expenditure (comprising social services, food storage, rural development and warehousing) is also likely to show a proportionate decline (along with a rise in population).

In order to improve the economic conditions of the bulk of the country's population and to reduce disparities in access to essential services, it is imperative for all states to take urgent measures to fiscally empower themselves. As past experience shows, higher fiscal deficits or larger transfers from the Centre do not provide an adequate solution to the problem of fiscal stringency. The solution lies in altering the pattern of expenditure away from salaries and loss-making commercial enterprises and allocating larger resources for development of infrastructure and socially productive sectors (see section [vi] on the 'Reform of Government'). There is no scarcity of resources in India to do what is necessary to do for the benefit of the society as a whole. What is lacking is the necessary political will to alter the pattern of expenditure away from activities that benefit a few at the expense of the many.

(x) Legal and Judicial Reforms

Judicial delays in India are now legendary. A delay of ten to fifteen years in settling cases of even the most blatant and clear-cut violation of law is quite common. In view of the long delays and the multiple levels of appeal available to any person or organization, filing a case has become a convenient way of avoiding a contractual obligation or conviction for a crime. As a result, all courts, particularly the High Courts, are now overburdened with pending cases. The effectiveness of the judicial system in protecting the rights of the people has been seriously eroded.

There are multiple causes for this state of affairs in a vibrant democracy like India. A person is free 'until proven guilty' and the burden of proof lies on the prosecutor. In principle, this is as it should be. Unfortunately, in practice, there are enormous delays at the level of the investigating agencies in collecting evidence. Corruption among witnesses and others is also widespread.

While the number of new cases being filed or appealed has grown exponentially over time (including those filed by the government and its agencies), there has been no corresponding increase in budgets, salaries and various other infrastructural facilities for the judicial system. Decisions on financial provisions and facilities are made by the executive rather than the judiciary itself. The decision to fill up vacancies in courts, as per the approved procedures, are also made by the executive branch. In view of the number of agencies involved in the decision-making process and the relatively unattractive pay scales at the higher levels of the judiciary, there are enormous delays in filling up important vacancies. Most courts are also understaffed and inadequately serviced. In line with colonial traditions, courts are in any case on vacation for several months in a year.

Another important reason for judicial delays is the plethora of legislative provisions on all aspects of national life, some of which are one hundred years old and internally contradictory. All ministries of the government, at the Centre and in the states, are keen to introduce fresh legislation and amendments to old statutes every time Parliament/legislatures meet. It is also an age-long practice, since the British times, for all Bills passed by Parliament/legislatures to include an omnibus provision that gives the unfettered right to the government to notify 'rules' notwithstanding any other provisions of the Act or any other laws in force. The rule-making provision, which has the force of law, provides sufficient scope for the discretionary and arbitrary exercise of power by the executive.

At the end of each session of Parliament/ legislatures, there is a solemn ceremony when the national anthem is sung to mark the occasion. On this occasion, it has become customary to assess the success of the session in terms of the number of new legislative Bills that were passed during the session.

The problems affecting the judicial system, particularly the question of delay in delivering justice, have been examined from time to time by Law Commissions, Special Committees, and Conferences of Chief Justices. Various recommendations have also been made to improve the situation. However, no effective action has so far been taken, and delays continue to mount. In view of the mounting delays, Fali S. Nariman, an eminent lawyer and former member of Parliament, has recently made several worthwhile suggestions to save the legal system from collapse.[7]

If India has to realize its full economic potential, and protect the rights of its citizens, the reform of the legal system can no longer be postponed. In addition to the implementation of the recommendations made by various Law Commissions and experts to expedite legal procedures, there is an urgent need to reduce the scope for appeals, adjournments and frequent hearings at different levels of the judiciary. In a computerized age, there is also no practical reason why all judicial appointments cannot be made in advance rather than with substantial time lags as is the case now. The executive branch can take the primary initiative for laying down the appropriate rules for appointments and promotions in consultation with the judiciary, which can be implemented by a high-level empowered committee without delay. It would also be appropriate to delink judicial salaries from those of the civil services and relate them to conditions prevailing in the legal profession. An initiative that the judiciary itself can take is to reduce the number of non-working days and the length of court vacations.

Let me end this rather long chapter with a brief recapitulation of the main theme of this book. As Indians, we can certainly be proud of our multifarious achievements in the economic, social, and political fields over the past six decades since Independence. However, it will be a mistake to rest content with our past achievements and ignore some recent developments that call for a change in the way we run our politics. Among these, there are three developments that particularly deserve to be taken cognizance of. These are: (a) the emergence of multi-party coalitions as a regular form of government; (b) the need to strengthen internal security to cope with global terrorism and domestic lawlessness; and (c) the widening of economic disparities during a period of high growth. In order to tackle these emerging problems, a ten-point programme of political reforms has been suggested above. This programme is by no means exhaustive, and there are certainly many more 'bright deeds to be done in India . . .'[8]

The well-known political economist and thinker, I.M.D. Little, has made an important conceptual distinction between the State and the government.[9] The State, according to him, is the sole and legitimate custodian of the sovereign power, and not the government of the day. The people as a whole are the constituents of the sovereign State, and governments must be accountable to them in accordance with the Constitution. In that sense, governments are the agents or tenants of the State, and no more. It is the primary responsibility of governments to discharge their duties in a manner which best serves the country's long-term interests rather than their own short-term interests of remaining in office.

References

1. Bimal Jalan (2005), *The Future of India: Politics, Economics and Governance*, New Delhi: Viking (Penguin edition, 2006), p. 135–37.

2. *Economist*, London, 22 July 2006, p. 61.

3. S. Paul (1999), *The Law Relating to Public Service*, New Delhi: Eastern Law House.

4. M. Harper (2000), *Public Services through Private Enterprise*, New Delhi: Vistaar Publications.

5. J.K. Ray (2001), *India: In Search of Good Governance*, Calcutta: K.K. Bagchi and Company.

6. Reserve Bank of India (2005), *State Finances: A Study of Budgets of 2005–06*, Mumbai, p. 24.

7. F.S. Nariman (2006), *India's Legal System: Can it be Saved?*, New Delhi: Penguin.

8. F. Max Müller (1882), *India: What Can It Teach Us?*, New Delhi: Penguin (Reprint, 2000), p. 31.

9. I.M.D. Little (2003), *Ethics, Economics and Politics: Principles of Public Policy*, New Delhi: Oxford University Press.

Epilogue

> If there is something wrong with India's democracy, it lies in the timidity of its practice. The road ahead for India will depend much on the integration of different concerns: preservation of democracy, much greater political focus on social progress (particularly in education, health care, land reforms, and gender equity), and democratic pursuit of poverty-reducing economic changes...
>
> We live in a world of many institutions (involving the market, the government, the judiciary, political parties, the media, and so on), and we have to determine how they can supplement and strengthen each other, rather than reduce each other's effectiveness.[1]
>
> —Amartya Sen

The opportunities for India to emerge as a global power of the twenty-first century has never been greater than now. As I look back, it is hard to believe that, not so long ago, India was a slow-growing poor developing country which was lurching from one crisis to another. It was dependent on aid to meet its perpetual deficits. It was also a habitual borrower from the International Monetary Fund to tide over its payments problems. Controls and rationing were common in order to minimize demand for financial and real resources. The same India, with a large and rising population, is now projected as one of the most important economies in the world (after the United States and China), and regarded as a role model of democracy for other countries. Among the factors which explain India's rapid transformation are the unleashing of entrepreneurial energy and changes in the global pattern of the comparative advantage of nations because of the technological revolution.

The challenge before India now is to seize the opportunities that lie ahead and realize its full potential to eliminate poverty, hunger, malnutrition and illiteracy within a foreseable future. Whether India would actually be able to realize this goal would depend on what it actually does, and not on what it can do. An important lesson of past history is simply that 'we shall continuously be surprised by seeing the unexpected happen. Nothing is permanent, particularly political development'.[2] Here, I am reminded of the cataclysmic and unexpected change that occurred in as robust an economy as that of the United States prior to the Great Depression of 1929–33. In his message to the Congress on the 'State of the Union' less than a year earlier, on 4 December 1928, President Calvin Coolidge had this to say:

> No Congress of the United States ever assembled, on surveying the state of the Union, has met a more pleasing prospect than that which appears at the present time . . . The country can regard the present

with satisfaction and anticipate the future with optimism.[3]

Looking ahead, while there is good reason to celebrate what India has been able to achieve, there is no room for complacency. As rightly observed in the passage quoted at the beginning, a number of institutions in the country, including the market, the government, the judiciary, political parties, and the media, will be involved in shaping the country's future. They can work together in cohesion to strengthen and supplement each other. Or, they can reduce each other's effectiveness through incoherence and disharmony. In this concluding section, let me take the high road and reflect on the positive role that some important institutions can play in India's tryst with destiny.

The most significant role in shaping India's future is naturally that of the government. Even when they are in power for a short period, governments have the authority to declare war, change policies, introduce laws, replace institutions and create public debt. Decisions of the government in these and similar areas can be crucial. Many countries have been plunged into persistent crises because of wrong ideology or unviable policies initiated by their governments. On the other hand, some countries with a poor resource base and widespread destitution were able to build a prosperous economy because of enlightened leadership.

In India, the primary task of the government at present is to improve governance. Notwithstanding conflicting opinions within and outside ruling coalitions, the economy is resilient enough to show a strong performance provided there is an improvement in governance and efficiency in administration. Irrespective of the shape of the coalition and the number of parties represented in it, there can be no difference of opinion on the need to improve delivery of services to the people through better administration. The government should take a realistic view of what is feasible, and then create an environment where there are no impediments to the pursuit of efficiency and higher productivity in different sectors of the economy, including the public sector.

On present reckoning, it is reasonable to assume that a large number of parties, many of them with a small number of members, would continue to be represented in government as well as Parliament. Several of these parties are likely to have a regional or caste focus with conflicting ideologies and interests. The positive role that these multiple parties can play in building a prosperous India can still be quite significant. There are three specific areas where an all-party consensus should be possible. First, all political parties must support the government's efforts to improve administrative efficiency and governance. There is no conflict in the pursuit of this objective and any other sectional or regional objective. Second, all political parties, large and small, must agree on the need to promote stability of coalitions, of which they are members, for a five-year period after national and state elections. This objective can be achieved if the anti-defection law, which is applicable to members of a political party, is also made applicable to parties and independent members of Parliament/legislatures which opt to join a coalition government. Third, each minister, irrespective of his or her party affiliation, should be individually made responsible for achieving annual targets announced by the government in selected areas of interest to the people (such as power, roads, education, health and guaranteed minimum employment). In case of failure, the responsible minister should be expected to relinquish office for at least one year (see Chapter 6).

In moving ahead, a major political problem—in part psychological and in part real—is the deadweight of the past. Much of the economic thinking on strategic issues was fashioned during the British rule. The post-Independence consensus was then shaped by the colonial experience and the pre-War realities of trading and investment relationships between industrial and non-industrial countries. Both these factors—the colonial experience and the pre-War trade patterns— strongly favoured an inward-looking strategy of development with the government being the primary determinant of appropriate development policies. Since then the world has changed, India has changed and the British have long gone. But, at the political level, our thinking about what is right and what is wrong has been slow to change, and there is very little accountability of the government for actual outcomes. I hope that in the twenty-first century, sixty years after our Independence, we will have the self-assurance to develop a more contemporary approach to the formulation of policies on national economic issues.

In the coalition era, the role of the judiciary is paramount in ensuring that the Constitutionally defined boundaries of executive action are not breached. A duly constituted government, after taking office, must work in the interest of the country as a whole rather than in the narrow political interests of parties represented in it. It is true that in the past there have been cases of the judiciary exceeding its jurisdiction and delivering some judgments which were not in the larger public interest. Fortunately, such cases have been rare and subject to further judicial review. Judicial delay has also been a matter of considerable public concern. It is of utmost importance that immediate action is taken by the government and the Parliament on proposals for judicial reforms, which require legislative or budgetary approvals. The rule of law must not only prevail, but also be perceived to do so by all citizens and others who do business with India. The primary contribution that the judiciary itself can make in this process is to ensure the most judicious use of its time by cutting down on appeals, adjournments, hearings and vacations.

As our recent experience shows, the most potent instruments for exposing cases of corruption and holding politicians accountable for their actions are: media, non-governmental organizations with a 'public-interest' agenda, and citizens. Their role and power to influence outcomes has been immeasurably strengthened by the adoption of the Right to Information Act. On several issues of public interest (such as environment, resettlement, right to information, flood relief, and high-profile criminal cases), the media played a vital role in raising awareness and putting pressure on government leadership to respond to the concerns expressed by public-spirited citizens and non-governmental organizations. One area which requires further attention is that of adequate follow-ups to ensure the conviction of politicians, bureaucrats and other civic authorities which indulge in corruption and neglect their duties to the public. Such persons are investigated, charged or even temporarily asked to relinquish office, but they are invariably back in power after a lapse of time. There is a need for media and citizens to be much more vigilant in ensuring that those who cause damage to the public interest are subjected to adequate and quick deterrent punishment.

I have no doubt whatsoever that if citizens and institutions involved in the process of India's growth and development play their roles positively and to the best of their abilities, no power on earth can stop India from realizing its vast potential and becoming one of the strongest economies in the world. The largest democracy would then have given its people their just rewards.

References

1. A.K. Sen (2004), 'Democracy and Secularism in India' in K. Basu (ed.), *India's Emerging Economy*, New Delhi: Oxford University Press, p. 42; and A.K. Sen (2001), 'What is Development About?' in G.M. Meier and J.E. Stiglitz (eds.), *Frontiers of Development Economics*, New York: Oxford University Press, p. 512.

2. G. Myrdal (1957), *Economic Theory and Underdeveloped Regions*, London: Methuen & Co., p. viii.

3. Calvin Coolidge, Message to Congress, 4 December 1928; quoted in E. Hobsbawm (1995), *Age of Extremes: The Short Twentieth Century*, New Delhi: Viking–Penguin.

Index

Abed, G.T. 114
Administrative Reforms Commission 186
Affirmative Action 75
All-India Conference of Chief Ministers and Chief Justices 101
American War of Independence 53, 54
Anand, Justice Dr A.S. 113
Association for Democratic Reforms (ADR) 99, 100
Authoritarian Political Systems 43, 45, 46, 102

Bar Association of India 178
Barro, R.J. 42, 64
Becker, G.S. 86, 97
Below Poverty Line (BPL) 75, 80, 81
Besley, T. 76, 96
Bharatiya Janata Party (BJP) 168
Bahujan Samaj Party (BSP) 168
Bihar 56, 156, 164, 177, 179
Bill
    Delhi Special Police Establishment (Amendment) 136
    Office of Profit 28, 133-34, 136, 208
    Women's Succession 138
Brazil 6, 49
Budget 35, 78, 133-35, 139-40, 154, 161, 173, 200-01
    consumer subsidy 80
    Session 27, 130-32, 136, 148, 208, 212
Business Standard 64

Cabinet 5, 21, 29, 57, 67, 99, 122, 144, 146, 155, 158-59, 166, 179, 205-06, 209
    approval 31, 71, 164, 223
    changes 222
    Committees 16, 69, 87
    members 24, 30, 59, 157, 163
    minister 55, 219
Central Bureau of Investigation (CBI) 95
Centre for the Study of Developing Societies (CSDS) 108
Chile 6
China 39, 41, 43, 45, 104, 235
co-operative banking 69
coalition 58, 67, 91, 158, 161-62, 168, 173
    governments 6, 10, 21, 27, 33-34, 66, 106, 155, 157, 182, 205-07, 211, 236-38
    stability 112
    multi-party 4, 9, 26, 28, 29, 59, 121, 144, 149, 151-52, 231
    politics 8, 53, 128, 139, 148, 181, 193, 221
    post-election 5
Comptroller General of India 78
Concurrent List 91, 190, 219
Congress Party 62, 148
    president 134, 136
Constituent Assembly 198
Constitution 3-4, 9, 32, 58-9, 83, 96, 97, 122, 133, 140, 143, 145-48, 153, 155-56, 174, 178, 181-83, 190, 196, 198, 205, 207, 209, 222, 232

Index

Amendments 3, 10, 12, 37, 75, 77, 91-92, 142, 175, 186, 189, 199
Articles 3, 189, 224
Bench 197
Preamble 53
protection for civil servants 223-24
Coolidge, Calvin 235
corruption 23, 24, 36, 88, 104-06, 109, 113, 115
causes 102-03, 217
Corruption Perception Index (CPI) 103, 114
effects 116-17, 168-69, 173, 213, 229
middlemen 44
of politics 97
political 3, 26, 37, 60, 76, 101, 108, 112, 118-19, 200, 221, 240
Council of Ministers 145, 154-55, 158-59, 164-65, 174
Council of States 70, 109, 195

Davoodi, H.R. 114-15
Delhi Human Development Report 227
demands for Grants 137
democracy 46, 55, 71, 102, 149, 185, 235
elections 47
European 54
Fundamental Rights 39
impact on growth 17-19
Indian 1-3, 8, 20, 27, 40, 52, 58, 62, 63, 65, 76, 109, 126-27, 141-42, 156, 229
inner-party 119
multi-party parliamentary 5, 23, 60, 211
Desai, M. 57, 64
dictatorship 42
District Panchayat Administrative Service (DPAS) 78
Dixit, A.K. 71, 72, 96

Economic Times 38, 89, 110
Election Commission 25, 26, 107, 131, 133, 145, 202-04
electoral processes 39, 109, 124, 201
pre-electoral alliances 68
state 56
state funding 199
essential public services 4, 14, 19, 23, 52, 160, 173, 228

Executive, the 59, 60, 137, 140, 152, 154-55, 173, 176, 179, 229
separation of powers 222

Finance Bill 28, 35, 132-34, 154, 208, 212
Finance Commission 82, 186, 191, 194
Fiscal
Budgets 106, 201
Deficit 85, 225-26, 228
deterioration 52
disempowerment 78, 81, 227
drain 116
powers 69, 224
Fiscal Responsibility and Management Act (FRMA) 85, 224-26
Five-Year Plans 15, 17, 191, 193, 215
France 54, 185
Friedman, E. 116
Future of India, The 14, 38, 202

Gandhi, Indira 175
Gandhi, M.K. 126, 128
Gandhi, Rajiv 169
Goa 56, 156
Government, Central 70, 80, 120
agencies 77
internal public debt 85
ministries 92
parliamentary form 5, 29, 157, 174, 186-87
policy decisions 29
predatory 72
presidential form of democracy 187-88
gram panchayats 21, 66, 75, 77, 79
gram sabhas 75, 77, 78
Gross Domestic Product (GDP) 85, 86, 117, 225, 227

Haryana 92
High Courts 228

India
agriculture 13
economy 2, 4, 12, 120
balance-of-payments 84, 214
foreign exchange reserves 225
inflation 116, 226
investment-income ratio 115
public-private dichotomy 52
reforms 13

Emergency 54, 58, 62, 142, 157, 206
famine 45
Independence 2, 14, 54, 62, 83, 104, 166, 174, 231, 238
pre- 57
struggle 58
industrialization 191
terrorism 11-12, 231
Indian Administrative Service (IAS) 30-31, 165, 168, 221, 223
Indian Express 64, 110, 153
Indian Institutes of Management (IIM) 161-62
Indian Institutes of Technology (IIT) 162
Indian Medical Council (Amendment) Bill 94
Indian National Congress 58
Indian Police Service (IPS) 31, 168
Inter-American Development Bank 38
International Monetary Fund 235

Japan 104
Jayal, N.J. 38
Jharkhand 56, 156, 177
Judiciary, the 32, 60, 98, 142, 147, 154, 156, 173, 176, 178, 222, 229, 231, 239

Karnataka 56
Kerala 49
Khilnani, S. 58, 64
Korea 41
Krishnamachari, T.T. 103
Kumar, A. 61, 64

Law Commission 230-31
Laws
Anti-defection 33-34
Legislative, the 59, 140, 147, 155, 173, 175, 222
Lincoln, Abraham 54
Little, I.M.D. 232
Local Area Development funds 112
Lok Sabha 7, 21, 25, 26, 68, 99, 108, 130, 133-34, 136-37, 149, 178, 198, 199, 203, 205, 207

Malaysia 104
Mauro, P. 115
Members of Legislative Assemblies (MLAs) 201

Members of Parliament Local Area Development (MPLAD) 99, 201
Ministry
Finance 161
Health 94, 95
Water Resources 163
Mumbai
bomb blasts 12
Mundra case 103

Nariman, Fali S. 230
Narmada Bachao Andolan 163
Narmada Control Authority 163
National Advisory Council (NAC) 134, 136
National Commission to Review the Working of the Constitution 128, 167, 186
National Democratic Alliance (NDA) 6, 161, 208
National Election Audit 108
National Rural Employment Guarantee Act (NREGA) 92
nationalization of banks 175
Naxalism 129, 213
Naxalite organizations 11, 120
Nehru, Jawaharlal 1, 126, 128, 175

Official Secrets Act 224
Olson 86, 97
Opposition 74, 122, 135, 139-40, 145-46, 148, 190, 206, 209, 213
Other Backward Classes (OBC) 162

Palkhivala, Nani 142, 182-83
Panchayati Raj 78
Panchayati Raj Institutions (PRI) 91-92
Parliament 3, 6, 7, 21, 32, 71, 98, 99, 118, 141, 151, 176, 196, 198, 203, 221, 223
adjournment 131-32, 137, 208, 210
Business Advisory Committees 211
debates 23, 132-36
diminishing role of 26, 28, 126, 143
Houses of 35, 122, 126-28, 132, 139, 160, 190
Members of 9, 25, 36, 37, 110, 112, 127, 134, 197, 209
proceedings of 130-31, 138, 150, 154, 207-08, 212
recess 146
role 34, 81, 140, 142, 164-65, 181, 219, 239

seats 54, 59, 123, 149, 204, 237
unicameral 199
Parliamentary Standing Committees
137
Planning Commission 80, 96, 186,
191-93, 215, 220, 225
police
malpractices 11
political interference 11
political power 88, 171
misuse 71, 72, 77
opportunism 57, 73, 74, 76, 77
pyramidal 20, 66-8, 76, 90, 123
poverty
alleviation 17-19, 24, 39-40, 48,
50-52, 68, 120, 160, 220, 235
anti-poverty programmes 77, 82,
169-70, 194
persistence 47-48, 114, 117, 129
ratio 49
President's Rule 57, 143, 144
Prime Minister of India 126
Prime Minister's Office (PMO) 165
private sector 14, 90, 105, 214
Przeworski, A. 42, 64
Public Affairs Centre 170, 214
Public Enterprises Selection Board
(PESB) 89-90, 172
public sector 14, 85-89, 104, 135
control over 87

Rajasthan 92
Rajya Sabha 59, 70, 109-10, 130,
133-36, 138, 150-51, 195-99, 209
Rao, Narasimha 6
Rashtriya Janata Dal (RJD) 144
Ray, J.K. 165, 221
Representation of People's Act 108-
09, 195
Reserve Bank of India 82, 96, 226
Right to Information Act 35, 77, 177,
217, 224, 239
Rural Employment Guarantee Act 141
Russell, Bertrand 20, 38

Sardar Sarovar project 163
Scheduled Castes (SC) 162
Scheduled Tribes (ST) 162
Sen, Amartya 63, 64, 234
Schleifer, A. 71, 96, 102
Singapore 41

South Korea 104
Soviet Union 104
Sri Lanka 49
Standing Committees 28
state legislatures 21, 110, 118, 128,
148, 176, 195, 203
State List 189-90, 219
Subramaniam, T.S.R. 60, 64
Sulabh Sauchalayas 218
Supreme Court 142, 143, 145-48,
163, 174-79, 197
Kesavananda case 142, 155

Taiwan 41
Tamil Nadu 56, 76
Tanzi 115
Targeted Public Distribution System
(TPDS) 79
taxation
by the Centre 192
indirect collection 116
without representation 130
Times of India 38, 64, 110, 153
Transparency International 103

Union List 189
Union ministers 3
Union Public Service Commission
(UPSC) 194
United Kingdom 54, 185, 203-04
United Progressive Alliance (UPA) 7,
208
United States of America 53, 54, 95,
123, 141, 179-80, 185, 190, 198,
204, 210, 235
Great Depression, the 235
Kelo v. New London 180
Roe v. Wade 180
Uttar Pradesh 54, 55, 168

Vajpayee, Atal Bihari 6
Varshney, A. 48, 50, 64
Venkatachaliah, Justice M.N. 96, 186
Vishny, R.W. 71, 96, 102

Waqf Board 209
We, the People 182
Weiner, M. 48
World Bank study 76, 96

Yadav, Y. 47, 64